# BIBLE CHARACTERS AND DOCTRINES

Onesimus to 'I Jesus'
E. M. BLAIKLOCK, M.A., D.Litt.

The Last Things
G. E. LADD, Ph.D., D.D.

William Jessup University
Library
333 Sunset Blvd.

William B. Eerdmans Publishing Company
Grand Rapids, Michigan Rocklin, Ca 95765

Copyright © 1975 Scripture Union
First Published 1975
First United States Edition July 1975

Printed in the United States of America

**Library of Congress Cataloging in Publication Data**
Main entry under title:

Bible characters and doctrines.

CONTENTS:
Cundall, A. E. God in His world. — v. 1.
Blaiklock, E. M. Adam To Esau. Crowe, P. The
God who speaks. — Scripture and revelation.
— v. 3. Blaiklock, E. M. Nadab to Boaz. Wright,
J. S. The character of God. [etc.]

1. Bible — Study — Text-books. I. Blaiklock, E.
M. II. Wright, John Stafford. III. Grogan,
Geoffrey.
BS605.2.B47        220'.07        72-189855

ISBN 0-8028-1472-7

SCRIPTURE UNION IN NORTH AMERICA
U.S.A.:    1716 Spruce Street
           Philadelphia, Pa. 19103
Canada:  5 Rowanwood Avenue, Toronto 5,
           Ontario

# INTRODUCTION

Each volume of Bible Characters and Doctrines is divided into the right number of sections to make daily use possible, though dates are not attached to the sections because of the books' continuing use as a complete set of character studies and doctrinal expositions. The study for each day is clearly numbered and the Bible passage to be read is placed alongside it.

Sections presenting the characters and doctrines alternate throughout each book, providing balance and variety in the selected subjects. At the end of each section there is a selection of questions and themes for further study related to the material covered in the preceding readings.

Each volume will provide material for one quarter's use, with between 91 and 96 sections. Where it is suggested that two sections should be read together in order to fit the three-month period, they are marked with an asterisk.

The scheme will be completed in four years. Professor E. M. Blaiklock, who writes all the character studies, will work progressively through the Old and New Testament records. Writers of the doctrinal sections contribute to a pattern of studies drawn up by the Rev. Geoffrey Grogan, Principal of the Bible Training Institute, Glasgow, in his capacity as Co-ordinating Editor. A chart overleaf indicates how the doctrinal sections are planned.

In this series biblical quotations are normally taken from the RSV unless otherwise identified. Occasionally Professor Blaiklock provides his own translation of the biblical text.

## DOCTRINAL STUDY SCHEME

|                   | Year 1                       | Year 2                        | Year 3                       | Year 4                              |
| ----------------- | ---------------------------- | ----------------------------- | ---------------------------- | ----------------------------------- |
| First Quarter     | The God who Speaks           | Man and Sin                   | The Work of Christ           | The Kingdom and the Church          |
| Second Quarter    | God in His World             | Law and Grace                 | Righteousness in Christ      | The Mission of the Church           |
| Third Quarter     | The Character of God         | The Life of Christ            | Life in Christ               | The Church's Ministry and Ordinances |
| Fourth Quarter    | The Holy Trinity             | The Person of Christ          | The Holy Spirit              | The Last Things                     |

# DOCTRINAL STUDIES
# THE LAST THINGS

# CHARACTER STUDIES
## ONESIMUS TO 'I JESUS'

# THE LAST THINGS

## Introduction

The subject of the Last Things occupied a much bigger place in the outlook of the earliest Christians than it does in the thinking of most Christians today. The passing of two thousand years has tended to have a soporific effect on the Church, except in times of special crisis. This ought not to be if we take the Bible seriously. The promise of the Second Advent of Christ should fill us with joy but also give us greater seriousness of purpose in the proclamation of the gospel and in our day-to-day Christian discipleship. The volume of material on the subject in Scripture is immense and so the studies have had to be selective, especially so far as the Old Testament is concerned. It will become clear as the studies proceed that all the elements in God's programme for the future are linked together and controlled by the Second Advent. The spotlight falls upon Christ, who is both the Hope of mankind and its Judge. The series ends with a selection of material from the Book of the Revelation, itself dominated by the disclosure that the crucified and risen Lamb of God sits upon the throne of the universe and brings events to their predestined climax, to the glory of God the Father.

# THE LAST THINGS

## Isaiah

### Introduction

Isaiah was one of the earliest prophets, prophesying during the last half of the eighth century B.C. (see **6**.1). King Uzziah died in 740 B.C. after a long and prosperous reign over Judah. While Amos and Hosea were prophesying against the northern kingdom, Israel, Isaiah and Micah directed their prophecies against Jerusalem and Judah.

The book as it stands is almost impossible to outline; it consists of a collection of oracles and prophecies whose history it is impossible to trace. For instance, the oracle in Isa. **2**.1-4 is found almost word for word in Mic. **4**.1-3. Isaiah is primarily concerned to confront God's people with the will of God for their present existence; but in doing so, he often speaks of the future, both in terms of salvation and judgement. However, his interest is not in the future for its own sake; he lets the light of the future shine on the present both to challenge God's people to faithfulness and to comfort them with the promise of salvation.

## 1 : In the Latter Days

### Isaiah 2

This chapter contains several brief oracles: the Kingdom of the latter days (1-5); God's judgement on an idolatrous people (6-11); the Day of the Lord (12-22).

The prophets seldom speak expressly of the Kingdom of God, but their writings repeatedly contain the idea of a time when God will reign over an obedient, redeemed people. Sometimes the Kingdom is concerned only with Israel. Sometimes the Gentiles enter into the Kingdom but in subservience to redeemed Israel (Isa. **45**.14-16). The prophets do not give us a detailed diagram of the future, but look at the future from different points of view. In the present passage, all nations will stream to Jerusalem to worship the God of Jacob. In the latter days (2) means in the indeterminate future. Later, however, it became a technical term for the messianic age (Dan. 10.14). In the New Testament, it designates the age of the Kingdom of God inaugurated in history by Jesus (Heb. 1.2; Acts 2.17). For Isaiah, the latter days will be a period in the future when God's law will be established, and an era of untroubled peace will ensue.

This day will also be a day of judgement. The house of Jacob has become rich; they have adopted pagan ways. With a haughty spirit, they have even filled the land with idols. All of this is the result of Israel's pride which refuses to humble itself before her Lord. The coming of God's day will mean the humiliation and judgement of a proud and rebellious people.

The third oracle is one of the earliest passages to speak of the Day of the Lord, which later became a technical term for the judgement of the world and the coming of God's Kingdom (Joel 2.1; Isa. 13.6; Zeph. 1.7, 14, 18; 2. 2–3). The Day of the Lord is that day when He visits the earth to frustrate all haughty and hostile powers, that He alone may be exalted in that day. That day means both judgement and salvation. The first oracle speaks of salvation; the third oracle emphasizes judgement. Both are necessary in the day when the Lord alone is exalted (17).

It is significant to note that there is no messianic personage in this chapter. Here, the Kingdom is conceived as coming by a visitation of God Himself.

*That day means both judgement and salvation—which for me?*


## 2 : The Davidic Messiah

### Isaiah 11

In Isa. 2, the Kingdom of God comes without a messianic personage. In this chapter, the Kingdom of God comes with the appearing of a Davidic King. In later Judaism, this became the predominant eschatology; and it provides background for the use of 'messiah' (Greek, *christos*) in our Lord's ministry. The word means 'the anointed.'

God had promised David that his son would reign for ever on the throne of his kingdom, and would be the choice recipient of the divine favour (2 Sam. 7.12–16). When this promise was not fulfilled in Solomon, it was understood to refer to David's Greater Son, pictured in Isa. 11.

The family tree of David has fallen but it is to be restored. The Davidic King will be an agent of the Holy Spirit so that he will be

11

able to judge with righteous judgement rather than by appearances or hearsay. The 'meek of the earth' refers to those who, in their poverty and weakness, place their entire trust in the Lord, in contrast to the rich, the mighty and the haughty, who glory in their own achievements. The King will be divinely equipped to establish God's rule. Our passage does not assert that this Messiah will be a divine being—the incarnate Son of God. It does indicate, however, that he will be divinely endowed to deal with wickedness and with wicked men. '... he shall smite the earth with the rod of his mouth, and with the breath of his lips he shall slay the wicked' (4). It is impossible to visualize exactly what this means or to imagine how this judgement will be carried out. Two things, however, are clear. The prophet does not expect that all men will be converted and join 'the meek of the earth'—those who in humility place their trust in the Lord. There will remain men who pursue the way of power, who will tread under foot any who stand in their way to self-aggrandizement. 'Wickedness' in this context is self-exaltation of men who gain wealth and power at the expense of others, whose trust is altogether in themselves and not in the Lord. A second fact is that the Messiah will be the agent of their judgement. This note of divine endowment to exercise judgement is echoed in the New Testament (2 Thess. 2.8). The same idea is found in Psa. 2.9 (see Rev. 2.26f; 12.5; 19.15). God is a God of love; He is also a God of justice and judgement; and unless all evil and wickedness is finally purged from the world, righteousness cannot prevail.

The scene of the establishment of God's Kingdom is this earth. The curse of evil and violence will be lifted from the realm of nature; men and animals dwell together in peace. Again, it is difficult to understand these words (6–8) with strict literalness; how can we imagine the digestive system and the teeth of the lion to be so changed that he will eat straw instead of flesh? However, the meaning is clear. Peace will reign in all the world.

# 3 : On That Day

## Isaiah 24

This chapter expounds both judgement and salvation. The reason for judgement is that God's people 'have transgressed the laws, violated the statutes, broken the everlasting covenant' (5). God called Israel to be His people, and gave them a covenant—an agreement. God promised to be their God; and Israel showed her acceptance of the covenant by accepting the divinely-given law and living in obedience to it. If Israel showed loyalty to the covenant by keeping the law, God promised not only to bless His people spiritually, but also to preserve them and bless them materially and politically. The problem faced by Isaiah and the other prophets was Israel's constant forsaking of the covenant. Therefore Isaiah pronounces divine judgement (1–12) which will devastate the land. That this section pictures radical destruction in semi-poetic terms is suggested by v. 12: 'Desolation is left in the city, the gates are battered into ruins.' The whole earth is pictured as being polluted and devastated from the historical judgement about to fall on an apostate people.

Beyond judgement, however, Isaiah sees redemption (13–16a). Israel will be scattered among the nations (13), but a day of rejoicing will come like the joy at harvest of the olives and vineyards. Songs of rejoicing will be heard in the east and the west as men lift up songs of glory and praise to God.

The historical redemption of Israel is not the last word. Beyond it is an eschatological judgement (16b–23). That our prophecy does not show the relationship between these several oracles reflects the nature of the written prophecy. This is a judgement that will fall upon the earth to shake it to its foundations (18–20). God's judgements will fall upon evil spiritual powers as well as upon wicked kings of the earth (21). Even the signs in the heaven will be confounded (23). The purpose of this final eschatological judgement is that 'the Lord of hosts will reign on Mount Zion and in Jerusalem and before his elders he will manifest his glory' (23). This is the ultimate goal of all Old Testament prophecy; the perfect reign of God in His fallen universe. We call it the Kingdom of God.

We should add that chs. 25–27 go on to relate other aspects in the final establishment of God's Kingdom. A messianic feast will be held for a redeemed people (25.6). Judah will sing a song of salvation (26.1ff.). God's people will be established in a redeemed land (27.2–6). Here we find the first promise of resurrection in the Old Testament (25.8).

*'Thy Kingdom come!'*

# 4 : God Who Comes

## Isaiah 35

The establishment of the Kingdom of God, which means judgement to the wicked and salvation to the righteous, is never pictured in the Old Testament as an achievement of man, or a process innate in the order of things, or even as an eventual and gradual conversion of all men. It is uniformly pictured as the result of a divine visitation, sometimes through the agency of a messianic personage, as in Isa. **9** and **11**, sometimes as a visitation of God Himself, as in this chapter. The key verse is, 'Behold, your God will come with vengeance, with the recompense of God. He will come and save you' (4).

The eschatological salvation everywhere in the Old Testament includes the transformation of the earth which has shared the doom of man's sin. The wilderness and desert places will be filled with flowers which will show forth the glory of the Lord and the majesty of God (1f.). There will be no more deserts or burning sands; fertility and beauty will characterize the waste places of the earth (6b, 7). Human weakness and frailty will be transformed into strength. No longer will fear possess the hearts of men when they see the salvation of God. Human afflictions—blindness, deafness, lameness, dumbness—will all be healed. The important point is that salvation does not here mean that 'when we die, we go to heaven.' That is, salvation is not the salvation of the soul or spirit; it is the salvation of the whole man and his perfect deliverance from the ravages of sin, and its setting is always the earth.

However, this total salvation is not an end in itself. It will only enable men to come to the Holy City where they will join in worship and praise to God. The prophet sees a highway—a Holy Way—where only the redeemed shall walk. The ransomed of the Lord shall tread this highway which leads to Zion, the City of God. They will march along this highway with singing, with everlasting joy, for they ascend to Jerusalem to praise and worship their God. In this worship they will obtain joy and gladness, and sorrow and sighing shall flee away. Here is another picture of the Kingdom of God: God's people, redeemed from bondage and human weakness, gathered in the City of God to serve and worship Him for ever in a redeemed earth.

# 5 : The New Jerusalem

## Isaiah 60

This is a rather difficult chapter for it contains a group of diverse oracles; but all of them relate in one way or another to the New Jerusalem of the Age to Come when God's Kingdom is established in the world. The Old Testament always describes the glories of the New Age in terms of Israel, the land of Palestine, and the city of Jerusalem. In Isa. 65.17, we are told that there will be a new heaven and a new earth. Rev. 21.12 makes it clear that not only the Church but also Israel will inhabit the New Jerusalem. The Old Testament does not predict the role of the Church in the consummation, but describes everything in the Old Testament idiom of Israel, Palestine, and her Gentile enemies.

Israel has been forsaken and hated (15), and Zion is pictured as a prostrate woman who is bidden to arise and reflect the glory of God which is about to shine on her (1). This glory will be unique to the people of God. The peoples of earth will remain in darkness (2); but they will behold the glory of God reflected in Israel, and beholding, they will be drawn to the beauty of the New Jerusalem. Israel will be gathered from the ends of the earth (4); crowds of exiles shall return to the Holy Land by sea (8f.). Israel shall no longer be rebellious but shall be righteous (21). God Himself will dwell among them; and the glory of the Lord in their midst will be such that they shall no longer have need of sun or moon (19–21). Many nations shall bring their wealth to redeemed Israel and to the Temple (5–7) and foreigners shall assist God's people in rebuilding the fallen walls of the city (10). The gates of the city will be constantly open that the nations may have access to the dwelling place of God (11). The Gentiles shall be made subservient to Israel and shall either serve her or perish (12), for in Israel God will be glorified (13). The glory of the New Jerusalem will vastly surpass the old earthly Jerusalem (17). The important thing, however, is that the New Jerusalem will be called Salvation and Praise (18).

Some Bible students insist that such prophecies must be taken literally, and picture the restoration of theocratic Israel in the millennium. It is better to use the principle of progressive revelation which sees the fulfilment of such prophecies in the New Jerusalem of Rev. 21, 22. God will surely fulfil His word but not in the exact idiom of the Old Testament. He will dwell among His people, both Israel and the Church (Rev. 21.12, 14); the glory of

God's presence will fill the city (Rev. **21**.23), and the nations of the earth will come to behold its glory (Rev. **21**.24). The permanent elements are the salvation of God's people, God's taking up His dwelling among them, the redemption of the earthly order, and the universal establishment of righteousness, salvation and peace.

## 6 : The New Creation

### Isaiah 65.17–25; 66.18–24

Isaiah's prophecies conclude with a vision of the new heaven and the new earth. The only other place in Scripture where such language is found is in 2 Pet. **3**.13 and Rev. **21**, **22**. This raises the question of whether Isaiah should be understood with strict literalness; if so, both the millennium and the Age to Come will witness new creations. It is easier to interpret Isaiah in the light of Revelation and recognize that these prophecies exhibit the language of analogy. The new, really indescribable order is described in familiar earthly idiom. The essential truth should be our basic concern.

It is important to note that all biblical prophecy sees the consummation of God's Kingdom on the earth. '. . . creation itself will be set free from its bondage to decay and obtain the glorious liberty of the children of God' (Rom. **8**.21). The New Jerusalem (Rev. **21**.2) will be the centre of the new creation. Joy and gladness will displace sorrow and weeping. Human existence will be so changed that to die at a hundred years of age would be like dying in infancy (**65**.20). That this is picturesque language is shown by the fact that Isaiah himself knows that death will be swallowed up in the new creation (Isa. **25**.8). Peace, tranquillity and blessedness shall prevail in all the new creation (**65**.21–25). As Isaiah has already said (**11**.6–9), the realm of the animal world will show the redemption of the new order.

The manifestation of God's glory will be a sign (**66**.19) which will be heralded to the ends of the earth. Nations shall come to witness the wonders of God. These nations will enable God's people, Israel, to be restored to their land (**66**.20), and Israel will abide as God's people for ever—for as long as the new creation endures (**66**.22f.). The New Testament tells us that the Old Testament feasts—such as the new moon and sabbath—belong to the 'shadows' which have been done away in Christ. This further supports the view that the new creation is pictured in analogical language of Old Testament times.

The prophecy ends on a sober note. The new creation does not mean the salvation of all men, and it is important that we take this seriously. Apostate rebels who scorn the Word of God and spurn the divine prophecies can have no part in the new order, but can anticipate only divine judgement. The setting here is probably the valley of Hinnom (*Ge Hinnom*), south of Jerusalem, which later becomes Gehenna.

### Questions and themes for study and discussion on Studies 1–6

1. If God's final salvation always includes the redemption of creation, what should be our attitude toward the natural world in which we live, including our bodily existence?
2. What was Jesus' attitude toward the created world? See Matt. 6.28; 10.29.
3. What changes need to be made in nature to eradicate evil?
4. The Old Testament describes salvation in terms of the nation Israel. Does the New Testament contradict this by teaching that the Church has displaced Israel? See Rom. 11.26; Rev. 21.12.
5. In the light of these prophecies, can the Kingdom of God ever be realized by human effort, even by the efforts of the Church?

# CHARACTER STUDIES

## 7 : Onesimus

### Philemon 1–25

There are three men in this exquisite little letter, Paul, Philemon and Philemon's runaway slave. Onesimus seems to have robbed his master, a Christian of Colossae, and made his way to Rome, which one of Rome's own writers called 'the common sewer of the world.' Onesimus sought hiding and anonymity in the multitude of Rome's slum-dwellers, was perhaps robbed in turn, and in desperation had discovered Paul. Perhaps Epaphras from Colossae had recognized him. He found Paul and found Christ, and the question of restitution arose. Paul solved it with austerity and sent Onesimus home, but sent him home with the gratitude he owed him and with a moving appeal to Philemon which forms the theme of this exquisite letter.

Apphia was, of course, Philemon's wife, and Archippus, not improbably his son. They, and the church which made its centre and meeting place in their home, were probably converts of the Ephesian ministry (Acts **19**.10). Archippus appears to have been something of a figure in the community, as witness Col. **4**.17. Only once elsewhere does Paul use the expression 'comrade in arms', or 'fellow-soldier'. The word occurs in Phil. **2**. 25.

What happened to Onesimus? For what it is worth we may look at a phrase in a letter of Ignatius written to the church at Ephesus some half-century later. Ignatius praises the bishop of Ephesus, 'a man of inexpressible love'. The bishop's name was Onesimus, and like Paul, Ignatius puns on it. Was the bishop the one-time slave in grand and useful old age? And is this why one private letter of Paul, prized through a grateful man's lifetime, found its way into the New Testament? It is fairly certain that the final collection of Paul's letters was made at Ephesus. Speculation, but it could be true.

Perhaps we may end with a quotation from R. D. Shaw: 'It was by his affectionate personal interest that Paul undoubtedly obtained his singular hold upon men ... The sunshine of his solicitude seemed to focus itself on each single life and to make that life its peculiar care. Great as he is when panoplied in theological armour, "sheathed with logic and bristling with arguments", he is greater still as he lavishes himself in the personal ministry of love, and seeks to win his crown in the growing grace and peace of the souls whom he has brought into the kingdom of Christ.'

# 8 : Last Word

## 2 Timothy 4.11–22

We have been a long time with Paul. We leave him today. His closing words are a cry of triumph and a plea for human friendship. 'Come before winter,' he tells the young man. He is to stop at Troas and pick up some books and notes. He is also to bring the cloak he left with Carpus. Perhaps the soldiers arrested Paul in the street. He had no time to pick up proper clothes, or hesitated to involve others by revealing where he lived. Dr. C. E. Macartney had a moving sermon on this verse. 'This is Paul's only robe. It had been wet with the brine of the Mediterranean, white with the snows of Galatia, yellow with the dust of the Egnatian Way . . .'

Summer was waning in Rome. The chill winds would soon be breathing down from the Apennines, and winter would close the seas to navigation. Paul's voyage and shipwreck showed what November sailing could be like in that stormy sea. We may guess that Timothy set out at once, to Troas, past the high hump of Samothrace to Neapolis, along the Egnatian Way, with a night at Philippi, across to Brundisium, and up the long Appian Way to Rome. Did he serve Paul again? Did he see him die at Cestius' Pyramid?

'Come before winter.' Haste was necessary, and Dr. Macartney put it well. It will soon be a score of years since that great preacher passed like Paul to his crown, and he would not object to quotation. 'Come before winter . . . Before winter or never! There are some things which will never be done unless they are done "before winter". The winter will come and the winter will pass, and the flowers of the springtime will deck the breast of the earth, and the graves of some of our opportunities, perhaps the grave of our dearest friend. There are golden gates wide open on this autumn day, but next October they will be for ever shut. There are tides of opportunity running now at the flood. Next October they will be at the ebb. There are voices speaking today which a year from today will be silent. Before winter or never!'

But suppose Timothy stayed to finish affairs at Ephesus, hurried to Troas and heard the words: 'No ships till April', waited there, and reached Rome at April's ending! So Dr. Macartney's sermon imagined. 'He goes to the house of Claudia, or Pudens, or Ampliatus and asks where he can find Paul. I can hear them say: "And are you Timothy? Don't you know that Paul was beheaded last December? Every time the jailer put the key in the door of his cell, Paul thought you were coming." '

## 9 : The Writer of Hebrews

### Hebrews 13

There is an unknown writer in the New Testament to whom the Church stands in deepest debt. He wrote the unsigned letter to the Hebrew Christians. Paul was once thought to be the author, though even the early Church thought, in some quarters, that it might be Barnabas. There are good grounds in style and language for supposing that Paul did not write the famous letter. Erasmus, Luther and Calvin disputed his authorship. Luther thought Apollos was the writer, a not impossible suggestion. Ramsay suggested that Philip wrote the letter from Caesarea to the Jerusalem church, after Paul had stayed with him, while Harnack made a case for Priscilla and Aquila. We do not know, but a man can hide himself behind his work, and sometimes it is better so. Whoever the writer was, he was deeply under the influence of Paul's teaching, and was a man with a deep knowledge of the Old Testament. He thought habitually in its imagery, and built his doctrine round it. He was a man of faith, and saw faith as the dominant note in his nation's history. He was a man of poetic mind, the creator, on page after page, of penetrating and memorable statements. His literary capacity is notable.

The recipients knew the writer (13.19). It is possible that the Jews of Rome were those to whom the letter is addressed. The synagogue was strong in the capital, and supplied a considerable section of the church there. If Rom. 9 to 11 was understood by them, they were educated Jews of the sort who might readily appreciate the kind of teaching which the letter contains. Does it somehow fit in with the visit to Paul in Rome which Paul besought Timothy to make before winter set in? And was Timothy in some way hindered by a time in prison? (13.23). Italian Jews in the writer's home town send their greetings, as though there were considerable numbers of Roman Christians who had sought safety in flight. No mention is made of the passing of Paul or Peter, though the reference to Timothy might indicate that the writer was close to Paul. The recipients were under persecution, a trial which had led to the defection of some of their number. More cannot be said. We are grateful especially for the eleventh chapter and the first verse which can be rendered: 'Faith is the title-deeds of things we hope for . . .'


# 10 : The Runner

## Hebrews 12.1–15

The writer pictures the stadium filled with the watching multitude of all the saints who crowd the previous chapter. Greek stadia can be seen in many places—in Olympia itself, by the Alpheus river, where the old Olympic Games were held, high above the temple of the oracle and the theatre at Delphi under the coloured walls of Parnassus, where the Pythian Games were held . . . Thousands crowded the long seats to watch the stripped athletes run, and this fine picture of the Christian running the straight race before a gazing multitude was one which would make any Greek recognize a familiar scene.

A race brooks no impediment. No man can run with flowing garments entangling the limbs, with 'ungirded loins'. The athlete had to throw aside all which might inhibit the fierce energy of his limbs, and the verse is quick to define the entanglement. It is sin which so readily spoils, slows the pace, defeats the end, and makes the runner finally a laughing stock to all who see his folly.

Like the charioteer in the race pictured in the letter to Philippi, the runner in the stadium could take no thought of the idle crowd, observing his pace, his style of running, his person. Of all men he had to be single-minded. What the multitude said or shouted, what they thought of his performance was irrelevant. All that mattered was the race. For this test, this moment, he had trained. In writing to Philippi, in writing his last letter to Timothy, Paul had this thought in view. The Greek race had its rules. It had its prescribed training. It was a test of all a man could do and be. It had one object—the prize. Indeed the Greek word 'athlete' means a 'prize-man'. Christ, in this bold metaphor, He the Great Runner, endured the contest and all its agony, for the prize set before Him, His reunion with God. Can the runner for Christ do any less?

Christ is his prize, Christ is the mark at the end of the course on which he must set his eyes and run, run, with every muscle in the utmost play, all the strength of life concentrated to one end. It is a fine word-picture, illustrated in much ancient art—and in modern life. With what patience, with what endurance do we run?

# 11 : James

## James 1

Who was James? James the son of Zebedee was martyred too early to have written the letter. The good Greek argues that the writer had lived some time in contact with a Greek-speaking environment. The language recalls that of James in Acts **15**, and there seems no good reason for disputing the assertion that James, the brother of the Lord, was the writer.

It is down-to-earth, practical writing. James sets forth the truths which are given to him in a rapid series of pointed remarks. His epistle is almost like a set of sermon notes, and if he could have but expounded them at length, as the bearer of his letter may perhaps have done on the writer's own instructions, no hearer would have found a contradiction between statement and statement, or between James and Paul, as Luther imagined. Indeed James' opening remarks are almost a rephrasing of what Paul says in Rom. **5**.1–5. James places his prime emphasis on faith, and sees as the fruit of the testing of faith the strong quality of endurance (3), the essential basis of mature character (4).

The latter half of the chapter is a splendid illustration of James' epigrammatical style. It is full of familiar quotations. Nor do the well-known words lose their flavour in a modern translation. Here are two renderings from J. B. Phillips' translation which strike home: 'Let every man be quick to listen but slow to use his tongue, and slow to lose his temper. For man's temper is never the means of achieving God's true goodness' (19, 20) . . . 'If any-one appears to be "religious" but cannot control his tongue, he deceives himself and we may be sure that his religion is useless' (26). James' sturdy common-sense has no use for words not backed by deeds, for mere profession without reality behind it, or for a so-called religion which does not transform life and build unselfish conduct.

Here was obviously a man who was weary of the sort of bent and spurious profession of faith, which had no supporting evidence in speech or action. He was a man with two feet firmly on the ground who wished to see reality visibly demonstrated. He was a preacher who believed in stirring a congregation to life. He hit hard and hit home.


## 12 : The Affluent

### James 2.1–3.12

James had a grand impatience and magnificent contempt for class distinctions. The Church today is paying the price for some of the regard for wealth and position which too frequently marred the Christian witness of some in Victorian times. Canon Adam Fox, in his biography of Dean Inge, quotes a letter of the Rector of St. Margaret's urging his friend to consider a West End rectorship: 'The congregation,' wrote the rector, 'almost exclusively parochial is aristocratic: there are no poor save a few hangers-on (coachmen and stableboys, etc.) belonging to the well-to-do residents. Thus the parochial work is limited to what may be described as "friendly and sick visiting" ' . . . James' first-century exhortation is sufficient comment on 1904. All are 'poor and wretched and blind and naked' before God. Andrew Carnegie, on his death-bed, asked his loved ones to sing, 'Come ye sinners, poor and needy . . .'

James in fact, seems to be considerably preoccupied with the problems of class barriers and social tensions in the Christian community, and we should be glad to know the situation in which he found himself, and the city of his ministry. Laodicea, as we shall see, had just such a self-satisfied community. This is one reason why James' message has some relevance today, when racial differences present problems in some Christian groups. James would have presented the obvious Christian solution with some vigour and downrightness.

And who shall say that the vigorous passage on the ungodly use of the tongue has no relevance today? For what purpose do we use the glorious gift of speech? The tongue can communicate the truth of God or the lies of the Devil. It can bring comfort, aid and blessing; or it can ruin a reputation, spread pain, distress and misery. It reveals as nothing else the true character of a man or a woman. Its movements can demonstrate a lack of understanding which might otherwise lie hid, or a wisdom which no action could readily reveal. What should a Christian do with his tongue? He should control it, never seeking to dominate in conversation. He should train it to say less than it might. He should never use it for falsehood, half-truth, malice, innuendo, sarcasm, unclean talk, or empty chatter. He should always use it where circumstances call for testimony, confession, or the word of encouragement. If he is one of those strange folk who find it difficult to say 'Thank you', he should train his tongue to utter the words, and deal with the vicious pride which inhibits them.

## 13 : The Businessmen

### James 4

James was a stern and vehement preacher. A sermon from him must have been a devastating experience of straight preaching and downright language. There is something of the Old Testament prophet about him. Consider v. 4, where he takes a familiar image from the Jewish Scriptures. Phillips forcefully renders: 'You are like unfaithful wives, flirting with the glamour of this world, and never realizing that to be the world's lover means becoming the enemy of God!' Loyalty is a demanding virtue. No man can be loyal to God and neutral on the moral issues of life at one and the same time. Hence James' burning insistence that faith must be demonstrated in upright living, sanctified lives and visible character.

In verses 13 to 17 we come near to picturing the congregation in which James ministered. It would not appear to have been a church purged or plagued by persecution. It was astonishingly modern, or, at least, early twentieth century, Christian but not as vigorously busy at the tasks of faith as it might be, a trifle easy-going, respectable and largely respected.

These verses, in fact, are a quite vivid picture of the successful businessmen of the Jewish Dispersion. Many of these expatriates were very wealthy men, and this is perhaps the reason that James finds it so necessary to speak of the difficulties of a mingling of poor and rich in Christian congregations. We catch a glimpse of the typically successful businessman, cosmopolitan, hurrying from city to city, carefully scheduled in his programme of buying and selling, confident, and boldly ordering the future. Such well-planned and organized living, said the apostle, could breed arrogance and a damaging self-assurance. Let such men hold lightly the things of life and the transient world.

Indeed, here is a word for those who, in this contracted, crowded, busy world, amid the many who 'rush to and fro', conduct their daily business—on crowded highway, on the narrowing seas, in the canopy of air. Life is menaced in new ways and James is right. Here are two verses to add to a well-known hymn:

> *O Lord, who art Thyself the Way,*
> *The Truth, the Life—to Thee we pray—*
> *On mountain road and freeway wide,*
> *Where sweeps our traffic's roaring tide—*
>   *Beneath the shadow of Thy hand,*
>   *Guard those who travel on the land.*

> *O God of sea and earth and sky,*
> *Beyond the paths where eagles fly*
> *O'er ocean vast and coloured land,*
> *Do Thou control the pilot's hand.*
>   *They cannot soar beyond Thy care*
>   *Keep those who journey in the air.*

# 14 : The Rich

## James 5

The first Beatitude named the poor as blessed (Luke 6.20), and the meaning of that paradox was that the dispossessed at least have a straight path to God, cleared of the arrogance, the self-confidence and the pride which inhibit all faith, all humility, all willingness to confess a need to be blessed. How few, said the Lord, of those who are loaded with the goods of this world's devising, can qualify for 'the kingdom of heaven'—the Lordship of God in their lives. They too easily develop the character of the farmer in the parable (Luke 12.16–21) who, in a poverty-stricken land and age, could think only of more storage space for his wealth, and a self-indulgent ease which took no thought of other happiness than his own—and that a happiness which conceived no wider scope than carnal holiday and a stomach filled with food and drink.

Rich men, said James, and they were becoming common in a Church which must have had more than one 'Laodicea', should sanctify their thoughts by taking account of the fragility and ephemeral character of their possessions. How eternally true are his words in this day of financial instability, of inflation, and those thousand economic ills, which rise in a thousand ways from human sin and extract all value from hoarded wealth, and destroy all confidence in material possessions.

And then before the ultimate reality of death, who is not penniless? Shakespeare put it well in one of those flashes of wisdom which illumine his very comedy:

> *If thou art rich thou'rt poor,*
> *For like an ass whose back with ingots bows,*
> *Thou bear'st thy heavy riches but a journey,*
> *And death unloads thee . . .*

Like the Lord, James saw riches as a small thing, possibly something to endanger soul and character, to be held of small account, to be used in faithful stewardship. There is a burden of anxiety in getting riches, there is anxiety in keeping them; there is temptation in using them, and mortal danger in abusing them. And there is a burden of account to be given at last concerning them. They are not an end of life, but a tool of living.

## Questions and themes for study and discussion on Studies 7–14

1. What can we learn about courtesy from the epistle to Philemon?
2. 'There are some things which will never be done unless they are done "before winter".'
3. When is anonymity desirable?
4. Single-mindedness in Christian life and service.
5. 'Religion and life are one thing or neither is anything.' (George Macdonald)
6. The tongue as a revelation of the man.
7. What are the ingredients of 'straight preaching'? Is any other sort of preaching relevant?
8. What did Jesus say on the subject of riches?

# THE LAST THINGS

## Daniel

### Introduction

Daniel in the Old Testament and Revelation in the New Testament are distinctly different from the other prophets. They belong to a class of Jewish-Christian literature called 'apocalyptic', meaning 'revelatory', because their chief purpose is to reveal the events that will occur at the consummation of the Kingdom of God. The other prophets have much to say about the future, but their main concern is with God's people in the present. The apocalyptists differ from other prophets in their use of symbolism to represent future events. Other prophets used symbolism sometimes as a vehicle for conveying their message (see Jer. 13.1–4; Ezek. 37; Zech. 6.1–8), but in the apocalypses, such symbolism as the four beasts (Dan. 7) becomes the main vehicle of revelation, particularly when seen in a dream or vision. The apocalypse of Daniel was imitated in a whole series of Jewish apocalypses, such as the non-canonical books of Enoch and 4 Ezra.

### 15 : The Smiting Stone

#### Daniel 2

In Old Testament times, God revealed His will to men by the use of various means which we seldom experience today. One of these was dreams (Gen. 31.24; 41; 1 Kings 3.5; Deut. 13.1). The present author has participated in one experience where God granted divine guidance by a dream; but this is not now God's usual way of speaking. We have the written word.

The dream given to Nebuchadnezzar had to do with a 'mystery' (18, 19, 28, 30). A 'mystery' in the Bible is not something dark and mysterious but is a divine secret or purpose in the heart of God which He chooses at the right time to disclose to men. A mystery is a revealed secret. This revelation had to do with 'the latter days'— i.e. the time of the Kingdom of God (Isa. 2.2).

The four parts of the great image are designated as four kingdoms, that of Nebuchadnezzar being the first. These four kingdoms have been differently interpreted but the traditional conservative position has been to identify them as Babylon, Medo-Persia, Greece, and Rome (see E. J. Young, *The New Bible Commentary: Revised* [1970], p. 691).

The important fact in the prophecy is that human kingdoms (which are based on force, conquest and war) are not to last for ever. In the latter days, they will be destroyed and the Kingdom of God take their place. The fact that the stone was cut out by no human hand is Daniel's symbolic way of describing an act of God. In some way, beyond our imagination, God will act to destroy the series of world empires which have arrogated absolute power and sovereignty to themselves. The fact that the stone smites the image in the feet—the fourth kingdom—but grinds the whole image to dust suggests that the succession of human sovereignties stem from a single source. Similarly, Rev. **11**.15 says that 'the kingdom (*not* kingdoms as AV[KJV]) of the world has become the kingdom of our Lord and of his Christ.' The growth of the stone so that it became a great mountain and filled the whole earth means that 'the God of heaven will set up a kingdom which shall never be destroyed, nor shall its sovereignty be left to another people . . . , it shall stand for ever' (44).

Some interpreters see this as a prophecy of the Christian Church which is identified with the Kingdom of God and is destined to conquer the world for the gospel. This idea, however, is not supported by New Testament teaching. The Church is not the Kingdom; the Church, biblically speaking, is the people of the Kingdom. The Kingdom is God's rule which must ultimately purge His world of evil, that His reign may prevail. In fact, the judgement of those who oppose righteousness is an essential aspect of God's reign.

'*Blessed be the name of God for ever and ever, to whom belong wisdom and might.*' (20)

# 16 : The Son of Man

## Daniel 7

Daniel 7 is a companion piece to Daniel 2. In this dream-vision, instead of an image consisting of four metals, Daniel sees four fierce beasts coming up out of the sea. The problem of the identification of the four beasts is the same as the four parts of the image in ch. **2**. However, this vision contains two additional features. The fourth beast had ten horns, one of which prevailed over the others because it was greater than its fellows (8, 20). It made war with the saints and prevailed over them (21). It spoke great things against the Most High and was allowed to afflict the saints (24f.).

If biblical prophecy is to be taken in strict chronological sequence, this should represent a greater king rising out of Rome who exercises unsurpassed power both against God and God's people. However, one of the outstanding characteristics of Old Testament prophecy is that it telescopes time. Its interest is not in chronology but in redemptive events. The immediate or near future is often portrayed as though it were the end of the world. (This characteristic is worked out in detail in ch. 2 of the author's book, *Jesus and the Kingdom* [S.P.C.K., 1965]). Thus the Old Testament nowhere predicts the Church age. The coming of God's Kingdom is everywhere pictured as the end time of Israel's history. This requires us to interpret the Old Testament by the more complete revelation in the New Testament.

The 'little horn' who blasphemes God and persecutes the saints is the Antichrist who will arise at the end of time. This is the first reference to him in the Bible. His main characteristics, here and elsewhere, are that he vaunts himself above God and seeks to destroy the people of God. He will be allowed to exercise his power for 'a time, two times, and half a time' (25)—a symbolic number for the prevalence of evil.

A second new feature is the manner of the coming of the Kingdom. One 'like a son of man' came with the clouds of heaven to the throne of God, received from God's hand the right to rule over all peoples on the earth in an everlasting kingdom (13f.), and then brings the Kingdom to the afflicted saints on earth who then receive the Kingdom of God and reign for ever and ever. The one like a son of man is both an individual and a corporate figure. He is a heavenly being in the form of a man who represents the saints on earth and brings the Kingdom to them. This is the only place in the Old Testament where this 'son of man' appears. This term later became a technical messianic designation. In fact, it was Jesus' favourite term to designate Himself. Again, the important fact in the vision is that God's Kingdom will surely come; it will displace all human sovereignty; it will be accomplished by an act of God or God's representative; and it will last for ever. The saints are to experience affliction in this age; but in the Age to Come, the Kingdom will be the Lord's and the saints will share that Kingdom.

## 17 : Foreshadowing the Antichrist

### Daniel 10

Chapters **10–12** of Daniel form a continuous prophetic narrative in which the foreshadowing of final events forms a central motif. In 168 B.C., a member of the Seleucid Dynasty by the name of Antiochus Epiphanes, king of Syria, tried to destroy the Jewish faith by compelling the Jews to apostatize under penalty of death. This story can be read in the Apocrypha in 1 and 2 Maccabees. If he had succeeded, it would have meant the end of God's redemptive programme, for there would have been no Jewish nation through whom Jesus could have brought salvation to the world. Therefore, the persecution of Antiochus is seen as a foreshadowing of Antichrist, who will attempt again to destroy God's people —this time the Church—at the end of the age.

Chapter **10** sketches the background of the rise and fortunes of Antiochus. Daniel was given another vision which outlined these future events. The vision, including that of Antichrist, has to do with 'the latter days', i.e. the coming of God's Kingdom (Isa. **2**.2). The glorious personage who came to Daniel seems to be the pre-existent Son of God (5f.). He was opposed by the guardian angel of Persia, but Michael, the guardian angel of Israel, came to help him (13f.). (The New Testament references to Michael— Jude 9; Rev. **12**.7—show that these 'princes' are to be understood as angelic and not as human dignitaries.) The heavenly being told Daniel that with Michael's aid, He had bested the prince of Persia, only to be confronted by the prince of Greece. Historically, Persia was conquered by Alexander the Great, and the entire civilized world fell under Grecian rule.

## 18 : From Antiochus to Antichrist

### Daniel 11

Chapter **11** continues the vision of chapter **10**, first outlining the events that led to the rise of Antiochus, and then describing the Antichrist.

Alexander will conquer Persia (3), but his kingdom will be broken into four parts, none of which will be ruled by Alexander's own sons (4). Two of these families which succeeded to parts of Alexander's empire were the Ptolemies who gained Egypt, and the Seleucids who gained Syria. The Ptolemaic ruler is called 'the king of the south' (5); the Seleucid, 'the king of the north' (6). The struggles and intrigues between these two are outlined in vs. 5–20.

The rise of Antiochus is pictured in vs. 20–35. He will not only fight with the king of the south; he will set himself up against the holy covenant (28), i.e. the law of God's people. He will profane the temple in Jerusalem, cause the burnt offering to cease, and shall 'set up the abomination that makes desolate' (31). 1 Maccabees 1.54 tells us that Antiochus erected an altar to the pagan god Zeus, thus profaning the temple with a desolating abomination. He seduced God's people to violate their covenant with God; 'but the people who know their God shall stand firm and take action' (32). 1 Maccabees relates how the Jewish Hasideans, under Judas Maccabeus, took up arms against Antiochus, and were willing to fight to the death rather than apostatize.

Beginning with v. 36, the vision looks forward to the one typified by Antiochus, viz. the Antichrist of the last days (see E. J. Young, *The New Bible Commentary: Revised* [1970], p. 201). Antiochus was an apt prototype of Antichrist because both tried to destroy the people of God and thus frustrate the divine redemptive plan. There are many details in vs. 36–45 which do not suit the historical Antiochus.

The main features of Antichrist are that he 'shall do according to his own will; he shall exalt himself and magnify himself above every god, and shall speak astonishing things against the God of gods' (36). This does not fit Antiochus. He will deny the usual human relationships; and he will magnify himself above every god (37). His god will be the god of war (38).

The final conflict between Antichrist and his foes is depicted in vs. 40–45. It is difficult to interpret the details. He will come to his end in a battle between Jerusalem and the sea (45).

*Evil men may have great power for a time but God has not abdicated the throne of the universe.*


## 19 : The Time of the End

### Daniel 12

This chapter is continuous with chapter 11. The time of Antichrist's rule will be a time of unparalleled trouble; but those whose names are written in the book of life—God's people—shall not be destroyed. Then will occur the time of resurrection. The righteous

—those who have been faithful to God—will arise to everlasting life; the unfaithful, 'to shame and everlasting contempt'. Those who in times of great persecution have stood fast and by their testimony have pointed many to righteousness shall receive the glorious reward of their labours; 'they shall shine ... like the stars for ever and ever' (3).

Daniel is then told to seal the book in which he has written the visions he has seen (4). This means that these events relate not to his own time but to 'the time of the end' (4). Verse 4b is difficult. It may well mean that men will travel about in vain to discover knowledge about the meaning of the times. It can be found only in Daniel's book. (See E. J. Young, *The Prophecy of Daniel* [1949], p. 258).

Daniel then asks about the duration of Antichrist's reign. The answer is that it will be short: a time, two times, and half a time. A popular view is that this is the same as the 1290 days of v. 11, i.e. $3\frac{1}{2}$ years. This is uncertain, for $3\frac{1}{2}$ years is $1277\frac{1}{2}$ days. It means simply that the time will be short. Verse 11 refers to the persecution under Antiochus as typical of the persecution of Antichrist. The two numbers in vs. 11, 12 are difficult. Young suggests that the 1290 days is the time of Antiochus' persecution, while the 1335 is a symbolic number designating the entire time of opposition to God's Kingdom (*op. cit.*, p. 263).

The book concludes with a promise of resurrection. Daniel will rest in the grave but will stand up in the resurrection at the end of days (13).

# Questions and themes for study and discussion on Studies 15–19

1. For the biblical meaning of 'mystery', see Rom. **16**.25f.
2. What is the common element between the establishment of the Kingdom of God in Isa. **11**.4 and Dan. **2**.44?
3. In light of Dan. **7**.13f. what claim is implicit in Jesus' use of the term Son of man? See Mark **8**.38.
4. Compare the portrait of the man in Dan. **10**.5f with the vision of Christ in Rev. **1**.13–16.
5. What characteristic does the picture of Antichrist in Dan. **7**.25 have in common with 2 Thess. **2**.4?
6. Does Scripture anywhere promise God's people safety from tribulation and persecution? See John **16**.33; Acts **14**.22; Luke **21**.16–18.
7. Apart from God's revelation in Scripture, do we have any idea of where history is going?

# CHARACTER STUDIES

## 20 : Peter Again

### 1 Peter 1

It is pleasant as we draw near to the end of the New Testament, to meet Peter again, mature, experienced, and a writer of no mean power. A map should be used to show the route taken by the messenger who carried this letter through a great circle of territory in Asia Minor. He landed, perhaps at Sinope, on the Black Sea coast, and left by the port of Nicomedia. Much of this territory was outside the limits of the evangelism recorded in Acts. Paul was prevented from penetrating Bithynia (Acts **16**.7), but it is known from the correspondence interchanged between the governor of the province and the emperor Trajan, which survives as the Tenth Book of Pliny's letters, that in A.D. 110 the area was so solidly Christian that the temples were deserted, and a problem created for the trades whose subsistence was dependent upon pagan worship—the situation of Acts **19**. Vast tracts of Christian activity went unrecorded. They go unrecorded still.

Peter addresses the Christian congregations as 'exiles' (1), and it must have been true, as it is increasingly true today, that the followers of Christ, Jews of the Dispersion, and Gentiles, increasingly found themselves alienated from the culture, if that overworked word may be used, in which they lived their daily lives.

Such exile was made endurable by hope, and hope, a living, vital force, was based on a risen Christ. Observe that the death of Christ is immediately linked with His resurrection (3). The writer was one who ran to the tomb in the murk of the morning, and 'saw the linen clothes lying, and the cloth which had been about His head folded up by itself apart.' (John **20**.6f.) He spoke of no myth, no delusion, but of an experience in history, which had transformed his life. Hence the paean of praise to God which opens with vs. 3 and 4, and runs on to v. 12. The writer is aware that persecution looms. Hence v. 5. The embattled Christians, which Pliny describes, needed this verse. We still need its assurance.

These converts had never seen the Lord in the flesh. They stand with us, and those on whom Christ Himself pronounced a beatitude. Link v. 8 with John **20**.29. Peter heard those words, and they never left him. It is a verse of rhythmic English in the AV(KJV), on which none of the translators has succeeded in improving.

## 21 : Peter the Preacher

### 1 Peter 2

In an earlier volume we heard Peter preach in those five cameo sermons in the first years of the Church. They were devoted to doctrine, exposition and pure evangelism. Almost thirty years have gone by. The Church has penetrated the world. Peter now, a man past middle age, has words to say to Christians.

Christianity was first called 'the Way'. It is a proclamation, but a proclamation not confined to the words of exhortation. It is also a manner of life, and half the impact of the Church upon the pagan world lies in the upright and devoted lives of those who belong to it. Consider a free translation of vs. 11 and 12: 'My dear friends, I do beg you, seeing that you are like aliens in a foreign land, to control your carnal natures which strive against your spiritual selves. Live upright lives in pagan society, so that your neighbours, slander you though they may as "evil doers", may see clearly your upright conduct and praise God, when the time comes for them to confront him.'

Peter's exhortation to godly conduct passes on to slaves. 'Household slaves, be submissive to your masters with all respect, not only if they are kind and gentle, but even if they are overbearing and unreasonable, for it is pleasing in God's sight, when, conscious that God knows all, a man bears his troubles patiently, unjust though his suffering is' (18, 19). The hideous institution of slavery lay viciously at the foundations of ancient society. The Church nowhere called the slaves to revolt, protest, demonstration, or to passionate claims to justice, and the freedom which is a human right. The apostles knew too well that violence begets its like, and that the doom of slavery, and the cruelty which it involved, lay in the slow, sure pressure of the Christian way of life. Paul sent Onesimus back to his master. 'In Christ Jesus,' he had already written, 'is neither bond nor free' (Gal. 3.28). Once man was granted freedom and equality before God, and once agreement was granted to the truth that personality, precious to the Father, was the possession of all men, slavery had no foundation on which to rest. A foul institution could not stand thus under-

34

mined. So with surviving shreds of slavery in another world. They will wither before Christian love, not before violence, arson, murder and rebellion. It is interesting to observe the wisdom which the memory of Christ, and the moulding of His Spirit, had begotten in the mind of the Galilean fisherman.

# 22 : Peter's Warning

## 1 Peter 4

The twelfth verse of this chapter begins the letter's final section of exhortation. The most reasonable dating of this letter is about the time when the fire of Rome in A.D. 64 and Nero's panic-stricken search for scapegoats initiated the first State-directed persecution of the Christians. To be sure the year A.D. 64 or its proximity cannot be conclusively set down as the time of writing. It might have been an even earlier communication. Perceptive observers could well have noticed, before the fatal climax of the fire of Rome, the growing antipathy of the proletariat and the mob's resentment against the Christians, a bitter spirit which had found expression in riot and misrepresentation in Ephesus (Acts **19**). 'A fiery trial' (12) was to fall on the Church, and Peter sadly marks it down as an emerging pattern. 'I beg you not to be unduly alarmed,' runs Phillips' rendering (12) '. . . as though this were some abnormal experience.'

Unfortunately, no century has been free of such spite and sadism. There have been more martyrs for Christ in the twentieth century than there were in the first, and probably in any century. The diabolical persecution which scientific barbarism has directed against mind and heart, as well as against the body, has written a sorrier and more sanguinary record in our own time than in Peter's. The ancient exhortation still stands. It is an honour, if courage can but rise to it, to suffer for Christ. Let but the conscience be clear, and no contribution of fault or guilt lend colour to the base allegations of the persecuting pagan (15). 'Steady then, keep cool and pray!' (7, Moffatt). 'Commit the life to a faithful Creator, and persevere in doing good' (19).

The pathos and power of Peter's words is enhanced by the fact that the writer was no cloistered preacher, uninvolved in the fate of those to whom he delivered his brave and solemn message. It is likely enough, if we date the letter aright, that Peter suffered along with those to whom he sought to give strength in the day of trial.

A persistent tradition in the early Church links the deaths of both Peter and Paul with the imperial policy established in A.D. 64, and carried out with some vigour over the ensuing years, at least until Nero's own sordid death in A.D. 68. Judgement indeed fell 'on the ungodly' (18), in that young sadist's suicide, and the grim events of 'the Year of the Four Emperors', A.D. 69.

## 23 : Peter and Mark

### 2 Peter 1

This chapter speaks of a great service which Peter rendered. Verses 15 and 16 perhaps refer to his commissioning of the first Gospel to be written, the narrative put tersely together by Peter's protégé, John Mark. A strong tradition, as we saw, connects Peter with the book, and there are many marks of Peter's personality visible in it. 'But I will see to it that after I am gone you will have means of remembering these things at all times' (15, NEB). The oral tradition, with persecution threatening the eye-witnesses, was not enough. 'It was not on tales artfully spun that we relied,' he continues, with a word for the modern tribe of 'demythologizers'. The Gospels are not mythology. They are without a doubt history, and investigation must begin there or be frustrated. Since the last century's attempt to place the Gospels in the second century ended in disaster, it has been impossible to dub the narratives myths in any sense of the word. The obstinacy with which certain critics continue to use the out-moded terms of mythology in New Testament studies, is a phenomenon found only in that branch of literary research. The methods of the 'form-critics' would run the risk of ridicule if applied to any other body of ancient literature.

Peter then reverently makes mention of one of life's great experiences which assumed deeper significance in Peter's life as the years went by. Verse 19 implies that, long pondering over the event on Transfiguration Mount, and the voice of confirmation which still echoed in his memory, Peter saw Christ more and more clearly in the light of the Old Testament oracles, which were available for all to study.

This leads him to pen a solemn warning against the distortion of that precious message by heretics such as those who were in the act of disturbing the Church by their 'private interpretation' of the Word of God. Scripture is too often the playground of those who seek tag or text to support their own view of doctrine. Peter, with his apostolic insight, saw strange deviations taking shape. The main lines of interpretation, wrought out by the Holy Spirit, through the broad awareness of the Church through all time, cannot be lightly disregarded. It is well for us to note the fact. There is always new light from the Word, but let the novel and the strange, and certainly the disruptive and the contradictory, be received as both should be received. Old truth may find new forms of expression, but new language must not damage or dissipate content or meaning. So relevant is this chapter. The strong common-sense of the writer comes through to us.

## 24 : Peter and the Liberals

### 2 Peter 2.1–22; 3.13–18

It seems quite clear from Peter's stern and passionate language, especially the reference to Balaam in v. 15, that the dissident sect under attack are those whom we shall meet again in Jude and Revelation, the Nicolaitans, whose compromising activities are likened to the policy of Balaam, who sought to break the rigid segregation of Israel from surrounding pagan corruption.

They are denounced in emphatic terms, the full impact of which may be best sensed from modern translations . . . Peter's old vehemence of speech, which once betrayed him, is now used to some purpose. The saboteurs of the Church were 'daring, arrogant, defiled, presumptuous, sensual, audacious, bold, scoffing, blasphemous, abusive, bestial, unreasoning, a stain and a disgrace, playing their tricks at your very dinner tables, with eyes for nothing but women'—all these are words and phrases of downright description culled from this or that version, and all justified by the uncompromising denunciation of the Greek text.

The words of the old Galilean again are tragically relevant. It is challengingly true that the rift between the Christian and the pagan world has widened. We live in a community which no longer disapproves of the abandonment of the Christian standards once observed and respected even among those who were not committed Christians. The Christian is no longer at one with the moral conscience of society.

The whimsical reference to Paul is comfort to those who find the Epistle to the Romans difficult. That letter is probably the document in view. It stresses, for example, the patience of God, which is the theme here (15, see Rom. **2**.4; **3**.25f.; **9**.22; **11**.22f.). On the other hand, it could be that Paul's letters were being gradually assembled, and read to the Church in many places. All of the great man's writings contain exhortation, passages of profound thought, and words capable of distortion. Some bent minds were busy at that mischief.

It was probably Paul's doctrine of Christian liberty which 'ill-informed and unbalanced people' (16, J. B. Phillips) perverted to their undoing. Taken with Paul's repeated calls for self-discipline, integrity of conduct, and upright living, no practice of permissive morality or unregulated conduct can be sanctioned by Paul's appeal for freedom from the law . . .

But that is by the way. We have said farewell to Paul. It has been pleasant to meet Peter again, feel his rugged strength and his power of leadership. And in this last page, he and Paul are once more side by side—great souls to whom the Church owes a mighty debt.

## Questions and themes for study and discussion on Studies 20–24

1. In what special sense is Peter evidence of the Resurrection?
2. Was the Church soft on slavery?
3. What is the psychology of persecution?
4. What marks of Peter can be discerned in the Gospel of Mark?
5. What should be the attitude of the Christian to so-called 'liberalism'?

# THE LAST THINGS

## The Second Advent of Christ

### Introduction

We have seen from our studies in Isaiah and Daniel that the Old Testament prophets devoted much attention to the coming of the Kingdom of God. In both prophets, the Kingdom is God's supernatural act, purging the world of evil and wickedness, gathering His people Israel into a redeemed land to enjoy untroubled the blessings of God's reign. The establishment of God's Kingdom is the goal of God's entire redemptive activity. While the idea of the Kingdom is basically the same, the messianic concept is very different. Isaiah sees a Davidic king arise from among his people, divinely endowed to rule in God's Kingdom. Daniel sees a pre-existent heavenly being who receives the Kingdom from God and brings it to the saints on earth. *These two diverse concepts are nowhere reconciled in the Old Testament.*

The Old Testament also has the hope of a suffering servant in Isa. **53**. He is neither a messianic king nor a heavenly son of man but an undesignated figure who redeems his people by suffering and death. The Old Testament nowhere shows how the Davidic King, the heavenly Son of Man, and the Suffering Servant are related to each other. They stand as three different messianic hopes. *The Jews of Jesus' day did not know how to relate them.*

In the New Testament, the establishment of God's Kingdom in power and glory remains the goal of God's redemptive activity. However, the New Testament reveals something unforeseen in the Old Testament. Before the Kingdom comes in power, it comes among men in the human, humble person of Jesus of Nazareth. In this new disclosure of God's redemptive activity in the person of Jesus we see a synthesis of the three Old Testament messianic figures. Jesus was the Davidic Messiah, the Anointed of the Lord; but His messianic mission was to suffer and die before He should reign in glory. He was the Son of Man who would one day sit upon the throne of glory (Matt. **19**.28), who would come with the clouds of heaven (Matt. **26**.64) to judge the world and to reign as King in the glorious Kingdom of God (Matt. **25**.31ff.). In such statements, Jesus claimed that He would be the one in whom the Old Testament hope was to be fulfilled.

39

However, the amazing fact about His mission, not clearly portrayed in the Old Testament, was that before He should come as heavenly Son of Man to establish the Kingdom in power, He had appeared among men as a humble Son of Man to minister, and to fulfil the mission of the Suffering Servant (Mark 8.31; 9.31). In this humble mission, the Kingdom of God – the rule of God— has come to men (Matt. 12.28). In other words, progressive revelation discloses that the Kingdom is to come in two stages: in the humble earthly mission of Jesus of Nazareth, and in His glorious return as the heavenly Son of Man. This is why we speak of 'The Second Advent' of Christ (Heb. 9.28). His first advent was in humility to suffer and die; His second advent will be in glory to conquer and to reign. Both advents of Christ are essential to the coming of His Kingdom. In some way, not made entirely clear to us, the coming of the Kingdom in power could not occur except by Jesus' suffering and death. It is our concern in these studies to deal only with the events attending the Second Advent which will fulfil the Old Testament hope as we have already studied it.

## 25 : The Approach of the End

### Matthew 24.1–28

Towards the end of His ministry, in full consciousness that death awaited Him, Jesus instructed His disciples about the events that lay ahead. Verses 4–14 instruct them as to the character of the interval between His earthly mission and the coming of the end. Jesus had brought to men the good news and the power of the reign of God among men. On two occasions, He had commissioned His disciples to proclaim and to exercise the powers of the Kingdom of God which Jesus Himself had exercised (Matt. 10.7f; Luke 10.8f.). They are to continue this mission beyond Palestine. In fact, the good news about the Kingdom of God must be preached in all the world, as a testimony to all the nations before the end comes (14). Jesus' disciples, and their successors, have a world-wide mission. This remains our primary task to this very day. When the entire world has been evangelized, Jesus said, the end will come.

However, world-wide evangelization does not mean worldwide salvation. The world will remain a hostile place. The gospel itself will not conquer the world. The course of the age will continue to be characterized by evils: wars, famines, earthquakes, and violent hostility to the gospel. Jesus' representatives will not find a uniform welcome. They will experience hatred, treachery and opposition; but they will finally succeed in their task of world-wide evangelization.

The age will end with two climactic events: the appearance of Antichrist and a final unsurpassed persecution. 'The desolating sacrilege' (15) refers to the hostile power first embodied in Antiochus and then prophesied of the Antichrist (see Dan. **11**, **12**). In Matthew, he is one who tries to usurp the place of God (15; see Dan. **7**.25) and to stamp out the people of God. He will launch the most fearful persecution history has ever seen (21; cf. Dan. **12**.1). Deliverance, however, will be sudden. God will shorten the days of tribulation (22), and in the midst of it, Christ will appear as the heavenly Son of Man like a bolt of lightning in the sky to save His people (27).

*What has v. 14 to teach us about our responsibilities in the light of the Second Advent?*

## 26 : The Coming of the Son of Man

### Matthew 24.29–51

We have seen that in the Old Testament, the Kingdom of God would be established by a glorious theophany—a coming of God —whose majesty would be such that it would shake the created order (Isa. **24**.23). In the New Testament, this theophany will occur in the person of the glorified Son of Man. He had already appeared on earth in weakness and humility to suffer and die; but God raised Him from the dead and seated Him at His own right hand (Acts **2**.30–33; **7**.55; Heb. **1**.3; Rev. **3**.21). As the glorified and ascended One, Jesus has already received in principle the role of lordship over the world (Phil. **2**.9, 11). However, His present lordship is not visible to the world but is known only by the eye of faith. This is why the most central primitive Christian confession is the lordship of Jesus (Rom. **10**.9). The Second Coming of Christ as the glorified Son of Man is essential to make visible His lordship and to establish it among men. His coming is described in terms of a shaking of creation (see Rev. **6**.12–14). It is impossible to imagine in concrete terms just what this will mean; but the Day of the Lord—the day of the coming of His Kingdom— means both judgement and restoration of a fallen creation. His main function will be to gather His people together from the four

41

corners of the earth to enjoy the blessings of His Kingdom (31).

Verses 32–35 are difficult. Many scholars believe that Jesus most clearly predicted the end of the age to occur within a few years (34). However, equally good scholars believe that 'these things' refer to the events of vs. 3–14. One thing is clear. No one can predict the time of the end (36). The important thing is to be awake. In the days of Noah, men were asleep even though Noah was preaching to them the impending catastrophe. So Jesus' disciples must be ready at any time, 'for the Son of man is coming at an hour you do not expect' (44). Jesus did not give a series of signs by which the imminence of the end could be calculated. If He had, men might say that His coming was in the distant future and therefore not relevant. As it is, He has left us in a state of indefinite expectancy. I do not know that His coming will be soon; I cannot say that it will be in the remote future. I must *always* be ready to meet Him. The key word is 'watch therefore, for you do not know on what day your Lord is coming' (42).

# 27 : The Call to Repentance

## Acts 3.17–26

This passage is taken from the second recorded sermon of Peter after Jesus' ascension. In the first sermon, Peter had proclaimed the resurrection of Christ (**2.24**), His enthronement in heaven on the throne of David (**2.30**) in exaltation at the right hand of God (**2.33**). In His exaltation, Jesus has entered into the new measure of the exercise of His messianic office and His lordship (**2.36**). He had been Messiah in the days of His flesh; in fact, it was as Messiah that He suffered (**3.18**). But He entered into His messianic reign only upon His ascension.

In Peter's second sermon, Peter stresses the fact that the sufferings of Messiah were in the plan of God. In fact, Peter says, His sufferings were foretold by all the prophets (18). Here is an important principle of Old Testament interpretation. Isa. **53** predicts the coming of a suffering servant who would redeem his people through suffering and death. In Isaiah, he is not designated as the Messiah; he is an unnamed figure. Messiah was a Davidic king who would rule in his kingdom. How could such a mighty ruler suffer and die? The Jews could not understand this. The two figures seem to stand in flat contradiction to each other. However, the New Testament *reinterprets the Old Testament in*

42

*light of the Christ-event.* Isa. **53** is now seen, in fact, to be a prophecy of Messiah.

The sufferings of Messiah present a call to His people Israel to repent and to turn to God to receive the forgiveness of sins. Such a repentance would result in far more than individual forgiveness; it would mean a new era of refreshment for God's people. Jesus has ascended to heaven and will remain there until His people repent and turn to God. Then God will send the Messiah in His Second Advent to fulfil the prophetic promises. In the context of this speech, which was proclaimed to the Jews, we must conclude that one of the events to occur before the advent of Christ is the repentance and conversion of Israel. Israel is still 'the sons of the prophets and of the covenant which God gave to your fathers' (25). Paul confirms this understanding of the passage by asserting that in God's good providence, all Israel is yet to be saved (Rom. **11**.26). The Old Testament promises for the final salvation of Israel are to be fulfilled, perhaps not in the precise form of the Old Testament predictions, but in their substantial reality.

# 28 : Waiting for the Son

## 1 Thessalonians 1.8–10; 2.17–20; 3.11–13

1 Thessalonians is almost certainly Paul's first recorded letter. He had visited Thessalonica and established a church there (Acts **17**.1–9). He had to leave the city hastily because of political pressure (Acts **17**.10) before he had been able to teach the new converts all they needed to be well grounded in the faith (1 Thess. **3**.10). Paul went on to Athens and Corinth, leaving Silas and Timothy in Thessalonica (Acts **17**.15). They finally came to him in Corinth with the good news that the infant church was prospering and was standing up well under persecution. However, they were disturbed about certain doctrinal matters, particularly about the Lord's return and the fate of those who died before that event. To meet these needs, Paul wrote 1 Thessalonians from Corinth, sending the letter by Silas (Silvanus) and Timothy (1 Thess. **1**.1).

The significant thing about these three passages is how casually the hope of the Lord's return is introduced in his thought. He devoted an extended passage to the subject (**4**.13–18), but the importance of Christ's return is ever in his mind. He reviews his ministry in Thessalonica and notes three characteristics of his converts: they forsook idols; they turned to serve God; they looked to the future to the return of God's Son from heaven (9f.). The attitude of expectancy must always characterize the Christian life. We look back to the finished work on the cross; we look up to the ascended Christ in heaven; but we wait in hope for the return of Christ to complete the work of redemption already begun (Phil. 1.6).

In the second passage (2.17-20), Paul emphasizes the joy and satisfaction he found in fellowship with the Thessalonian believers. After being compelled to leave them he longed to return to them, but 'Satan hindered us.' However, even though immediate fellowship may be broken on earth, Paul takes delight in the anticipation of a restored fellowship at the return of Christ when he will experience great joy because they will meet together in the presence of Christ. It is significant that the focus of his anticipation of restored fellowship is not death; it awaits the return of the Lord when earth's broken relationships will all be healed.

The third passage (3.11-13) is a prayer that God will preserve his beloved friends in Thessalonica until the return of the Lord. The word Paul uses is Parousia which means 'presence' or 'arrival'. Since His ascension, Christ is absent from His people, in heaven. His Second Advent will mean His return to be for ever with His people. He will come 'with all his saints' (13). 'Saints' is literally 'holy ones' and Zech. 14.5 speaks of the coming of God with all His holy ones. The New Testament often refers to the return of Christ accompanied by His holy angels (2 Thess. 1.7; Mark 8.38; Matt. 16.27; 25.31). Throughout the New Testament, this is the hope of the believer: to meet face to face the One in whom, not having seen, he has believed (1 John 3.2).

'And every one who thus hopes in him purifies himself as he is pure' (1 John 3.3).

# 29 : The Rapture and the Resurrection

## 1 Thessalonians 4.13-18

Paul had preached in Thessalonica the Parousia or Second Advent of Christ as the hope of the believer. Apparently, Paul proclaimed the return of the Lord as an event whose date was unknown but one which could occur at any time. After Paul's departure from Thessalonica, several believers had died, and the question naturally arose as to what would happen to the dead in Christ at the Parousia.

Paul here deals with this problem. He says that those who have died will not be left behind; those living will not precede the dead. (Note that the AV[KJV]'s 'prevent' is an archaic word.) Three events will mark this great day. The first is the Second Advent of Christ. He will sound a cry of command to wake the dead; the archangel will also sound a call, which will be reinforced by the trumpet's sound (see Matt. 24.31). This is symbolic language to describe the awakening of the dead.

The second event is that 'the dead in Christ will rise first', i.e. before anything happens to the living believers. In the next section of our lessons we will study the resurrection in detail. Suffice it here to say that the New Testament says very little about the intermediate state. It says only that death means absence from the body to be with the Lord (Phil. 1.23; 2 Cor. 5.8). However, this is a temporary situation which is not the fulfilment of the Christian hope. The goal of the Christian existence is not 'to die and go to heaven', as it is often expressed, but rather, it is the resurrection of the body at the Second Advent of Christ. We shall see in the next section that while it is the mortal body that is raised, the body is glorified and transformed so as to be no longer a mortal, physical body.

Immediately after the resurrection of the dead, the living saints 'are caught up together with them in the clouds to meet the Lord in the air' (17). This is usually spoken of as the 'rapture' of the Church, from the Latin *rapiemur*, 'we shall be caught up'. This is Paul's way of saying that the living saints will pass from mortality to immortality without passing through death. The idea of being caught up in the air means the putting on of the glorified resurrected body which is no longer limited by the laws of space and gravity. The Bible nowhere tells us anything about the actual constitution of the body. The best commentary on it is 1 Cor. 15.49: 'Just as we have borne the image of the man of dust (Adam), we shall also bear the image of the man of heaven (Christ).' The important thing is that it is still bodily existence, but a body adapted to an entirely new order of existence: the glorious Kingdom of God.

# 30 : The Coming of the Day

## 1 Timothy 6.13–16; 2 Timothy 4.6–8

These two letters belong to the so-called 'Pastoral Epistles' and were written towards the end of Paul's life to give pastoral advice to one of his beloved assistants. They show that even as he faced death, the Second Advent of Christ remained his joy and hope.

Paul exhorts Timothy to 'keep the commandment unstained and free from reproach' (14). The commandment cannot be narrowly defined but must be identical with 'the faith' (12) which is synonymous with the gospel. The ground for faithfulness is that at the appearing of our Lord Jesus Christ, Timothy and all others like him must give an account of their stewardship to their Lord. The appearing of Christ will occur 'at the proper time' (15), i.e. when God decrees it. The return of Christ is still a living hope that provides a dynamic impetus to faithful service; but its time is known only to God.

The passage from 2 Timothy is among the last words we possess from the apostle's pen. He is facing death by martyrdom, for he is in his second imprisonment in Rome. He views his death as a sacrifice. He briefly reviews his life and mission and is satisfied that he has been faithful to his calling. Then he looks forward, and his hope is not to a reward after death in the intermediate state, but at the Day of the Lord. The expression 'the Day' is a technical term meaning the Day of the Lord (1 Thess. 5.2), the Day of Christ (Phil. 1.10), the Day of the Lord Jesus Christ (1 Cor. 1.8), or the Day of God (2 Pet. 3.12). It is the day of Christ's Second Advent. Some scholars have tried to find several different days in this terminology, but they are simply different ways of describing the same Day. That Day will be not only the time of resurrection but also the time of rewards. Christ will be the faithful judge who will reward Paul with the 'crown of righteousness' (8). This means that God will give a reward, here likened to the wreath won by victors in athletic contests, in recognition of a righteous life. This reward is reserved, not only for the great apostle Paul, but also for all of Jesus' followers who, like Timothy, have kept the faith and have lived their life in constant anticipation of the Day when they would meet their Lord. Such may be said to 'have loved his appearing'. See 1 John 3.2f.

**Questions and themes for study and discussion on Studies 25–30**

1. What do you understand by Jesus' affirmation that the Kingdom of God *has come* in His person and mission? (Matt. **12**.28).
2. How does one receive the Kingdom of God? (Mark **10**.15; see Matt. **13**.18ff.).
3. Why is the realization of God's Kingdom—God's rule—incomplete apart from the Second Advent of Christ?
4. What relevance does Matt. **24**.14 have for the Church's understanding of its mission in the world?
5. What does it mean to 'watch' for the Lord's return? See Matt. **24**.42; 1 Thess. **5**.6.
6. In view of Acts **3**.17–26, what should be the attitude of Christians towards Jewish people?

# CHARACTER STUDIES

## 31 : Jude's Epistle

### Jude 1–25

We shall read Jude before John, because he wrote at least before John wrote his first letter. Jude's tract against emerging heresy belongs to the same order of writing as the second and third letters of John, except that Jude writes to all the community of Christ, while John, although with a whole congregation in mind, addressed primarily in his second and third letters, one person. There was a general alarm about heresy at the time, as we have seen in reading the second letter of Peter. There is also striking similarity between 2 Peter and Jude to the point of actual quotation. It would appear that Jude quoted Peter rather than the reverse, assuming again that the traditional date for the death of Peter is near the truth. The name Jude, or Judas, was made common by Judas Maccabaeus, the Jewish resistance-hero and freedom-fighter, and six of that name are mentioned in the New Testament, two of them actually in the apostles' band. Jude decribes himself as 'brother of James'. There was only one James who could be referred to without further definition after the death of the apostle James, and that was James 'the Lord's brother' (Gal. 1.19). If, then, Jude was the brother of James, he was also the brother of the Lord, perhaps the youngest (Matt. 13.55), or the next to youngest of the family (Mark 6.3). Both James and Jude were missionaries, travelling with their families (1 Cor. 9.5). We know no more.

James seems to have decided to write a doctrinal treatise on salvation (3) and it would have made an interesting contribution to Christian literature. And evidentially a most significant one, for James and Jude did not, in His lifetime, accept their brother's claims (John 7.5). Could there be a more striking proof of the historicity of the Resurrection, than the ascription of saviourhood and divinity to Jesus by James and Judas of His own household? Jude was turned from an original plan, which may have been carried out in a later letter lost to us, by the sudden need to write, like Peter, and later John also, in stern denunciation of theological corruption. The form taken by the heresy was no doubt the misinterpretation of Paul's salutary doctrine of Christian liberty

(4) by men with 'no true acceptance of God, but who abuse his grace as an excuse for immorality'.

And so Judas, of better fame, comes briefly into view as the New Testament ends—a valiant fighter, just glimpsed in the fray.


## 32 : John at Work

### 2 John 1–13

John's second and third letters preceded the first in the earliest ordered collection. Hence the present sequence. God spoke and speaks through the simplicities of life, and this little letter is like thousands of others which have survived among the papyri of Egypt. Scholars too prone to pass by the plain meaning of a text, have also imagined that the 'elect lady' is a church. Such a disguised form of communication would be more proper in Revelation. 'Lady', in Greek is 'Kuria', and this word, as many contexts in the papyri show, can be a proper name. This letter is therefore in all probability addressed to 'Kuria, a Christian'. Since Kuria is the Greek for the Hebrew Martha, it has been suggested, but with no possibility of proof, that we have here a flash of light on the later years of Lazarus' and Mary's sister, a widow with a grown-up family. Travel was easy in the first century, and the Bethany family could easily have sought refuge in Asia. It appears that some of Kuria's children had visited cousins, children of a deceased sister (Mary?) who lived in Ephesus (13). John had found them fine Christians, and sends his and the cousins' greetings to Kuria in her home town. Here she used her home (10) as a Christian centre, as did Nympha at Colossae (Col. 4.15) and Philemon of the same city (Philem. 2). It is interesting to observe the apostle at his pastoral work, and to see the continuing role of faithful women in the early Christian communities. He takes occasion to sum up his favourite message: 'The commandment is love; love is walking according to the commandments: His commandments are summed up in a word—love'. The gracious tone of the little letter, penned, no doubt, in the midst of multitudinous duties and distractions, is an illustration of the love which John preached.

Further communication the elder left until a personal visit— always a wise proceeding. To meet and discuss a question at issue is likely to be a safer and more gracious process than the laying down of firm principles for others' interpretation, or possible mistaken emphasis. To meet face to face is the surer way to understand, and to allow the free play of the third Person, who is always present 'where two or three are gathered in his name'. The great R. W. Dale of Birmingham had reservations about Moody until he heard him speak, and was won by the grace and yearning of the evangelist's appeal. John shrinks from any diminution in Christian joy (12), and so postpones much serious discussion until a visit which was part of his pastoral plan. The whole letter is a fascinating glimpse into the activities of unrecorded years in the city where Paul had founded a church, and Timothy had organized it.


## 33 : John the Pastor

### 3 John 1–15

Gaius was a common name, and several who bear it appear in the New Testament. Gaius of Corinth (Rom. **16**.23; 1 Cor. **1**.14), is said to have been John's amanuensis when he wrote his Gospel, and he may be the Gaius commended in this letter. A Gaius is said to have been placed in charge of the church at Pergamum by John, and this may also be a reference to 'the well-beloved Gaius'. In v. 3 John mentions the source of his information about the good man. The verse suggests much going and coming from Ephesus of itinerant teachers and officials of the church, and the existence in Asia of a closely-knit organization. Hospitality to such ministers of Christ was a duty, and in v. 5 Gaius' faultless record is praised. A sure means of bringing blessing to a home, and of building some Christian ideals in its children, is to entertain good men and women. But let the adjective be emphasized. In both of these small letters, the existence of those who abused the hospitality of the Christian community is implied. Let hospitality, like all else, be mixed with discernment. In v. 8 the worth and place of the Christian home in such a ministry is stressed. William Carey once compared his missionary work and enterprise to the exploration of a mine. He said: 'I will go down if you will hold the ropes.' A sound core of Christian hospitality was vital to the witness of the church, but John wished to have a sharp distinction drawn between the parasites of highway and pavement and his itinerant teachers and preachers.

Trouble had arisen in Gaius' congregation, and the ringleader was one Diotrephes, probably a rich layman. The division may have been on some such doctrinal rift as that which weakened

Corinth (1 Cor. 1.10–17). At all events, the offending Diotrephes was a domineering man, who objected to the hospitality which Gaius had given to visiting evangelists, who had John's approval (9f.). John saw the harsh treatment meted out to worthy men as an attack upon himself. The group had reported the incident in Ephesus, and this epistle was the result, sent by the hand of Demetrius, and promising a personal investigation. John does not threaten any form of excommunication, only a confrontation. Demetrius is set in contrast with the tongue-free slanderer Diotrephes. He was not known to Gaius, and so has this letter of commendation. There is threefold testimony to his worth, that of the Ephesian Christians, that of 'the Truth', which surely means that Demetrius' life exemplified the reality of the Christ of whom he spoke, and that of the apostle and his immediate colleagues. The letter ends as the second letter did, a fact which suggests that the two documents were written about the same time and just before a visitational circuit. The worth of the letter historically consists in the light it throws on the early Church.


## 34 : John the Beloved

### 1 John 1

We have met Peter in his epistles. We shall now meet his friend in extreme old age. We shall see John, and the Church at the end of the century. The first of these three letters, so revealing, so penetrating, was in all probability written to accompany the Fourth Gospel. The New Testament was approaching completion. The Synoptic Gospels were in circulation; the writings of Luke were generally known; the letters of Paul, Peter, Jude, and James were in common and already cherished possession of the Church. And now, with the ministry of Paul behind, with half a century of Christian experience to shape the life and reveal the problems of the Christian community, and with a life-time of pondering over those glorious three years in Palestine to enrich his memory, John felt the deep urge to write his Gospel. That precious book was to close the New Testament, and was to show Christ afresh against the background of the years, and in relation to the now completed body of Christian truth. If the letter was written to accompany and to introduce the Gospel, the two must be read side by side in mutual and fruitful commentary.

The letter dealt more directly with the spiritual problems of the hour, and attacked error with a directness which would have been out of place in the Gospel. It applied to the moment's need the truths developed in the Gospel. It formed, in a manner, a sermon upon it. And the letter, together with the Gospel, cast the only light we have upon the last thirty years of the first century.

We find more than history there; we shall find the author, and to gain some notion of the mind and heart of one who walked with Christ, half a century beyond those moving years, is fascinatingly interesting. We know little of the apostle's life over those fifty years, but enough to follow its main outlines. Several references in the Book of Acts and one in Galatians, suggest that he remained in Jerusalem until about A.D. 50. It is possible that he was in Rome at the time of the Neronian persecution in the middle sixties, and very probable that, after the martyrdom of Peter and Paul, he went to Ephesus. His mature ministry was certainly exercised here, and the 'seven churches of Revelation' were no doubt his 'circuit'. Revelation itself was written during this period.


## 35 : The Heretics

### John 1.1–18

John's Gospel, John's letters, would not have been written had it not been for the emergence of a subtle attack on the Church. It thus appears that we must treat Cerinthus and the Nicolaitans as 'characters of Scripture', but must fortify the mind before describing them by reading John's first eighteen verses in which he tells what the whole Testament is about.

Irenaeus, who knew Polycarp, the disciple of John, wrote that John set out 'to remove the error sown among men by Cerinthus, and much earlier by those who are called Nicolaitans'.

Who were these sectaries? Cerinthus appears to have been a forerunner of those, who, in the second century, were called Gnostics. Their doctrine was a species of theosophy. The 'deep things' of the gospel were for the enlightened few, for 'those who knew', for that is what the word Gnostic means. They were a sort of self-constituted spiritual *élite*, exempt from the rules of holy conduct which were observed by the simple souls who took the gospel literally. Cerinthus, clearly of their ancestry, had some special notions about the nature of Christ. He distinguished, in fact, Christ from Jesus. Jesus was the human son of Joseph and Mary into whom the Son came at the Baptism, only to withdraw before the Crucifixion. It was Jesus who died, not Christ. John clearly has this pernicious error in mind in the first chapters of the letter.

And the Nicolaitans? It is quite clear to any careful reader of the New Testament that there was a group in the early Church whose muddy trail begins in the First Epistle to Corinth and runs through Jude, Peter and John to the Apocalypse. They are called variously the followers of Balaam and Cain (Jude 11; Rev. 2.14), and both terms are illuminating. It will be readily seen, if the Old Testament background is remembered, that we have in the Nicolaitans those who saw little ethical compulsion in the faith of Christ. In Corinth they probably frequented the temple of Aphrodite, everywhere they attended the guild-feasts, conformed, no doubt, to the State Caesar-cult, and sought to keep a compromising foot in both worlds. Clement calls them 'dissolute he-goats', and no lower term can be found in the vocabulary of ancient abuse. All this is suggested by the reference to Balaam. And Cain suggests the bloodless altar, flower-decked, the mark and emblem of a religion void of moral sternness. Jude and Second Peter should be read by those who seek to understand the danger which lay in this vicious movement. Writing to Thyatira, John calls one of their leaders Jezebel (Rev. 2. 20) and that name is redolent of a ruinous alliance between Israel and Tyre, a mingling of light and darkness, of God and Belial. Such were the forms of the pagan attack on Christianity—an intellectualism which emptied the gospel of its content, and a libertinism which soiled its testimony.

Their only use in history was that they provoked the writings of John's old age.


## *36 : John and His Children

### 1 John 2.1–17

In a sudden burst of tenderness the old apostle turns from 'we' to 'I', and addresses his readers with the affectionate vocative which he is to repeat six times. No one had a better right than the last survivor of the Twelve to look upon himself as the father of the family of faith. Those who seek long and intimate study of the mind of John should note and seek in this letter the thronging echoes of the Gospel. It is often possible to seize and to enjoy the passing images in that rich store. Here he is remembering the strange, tense atmosphere in the room which Judas had just left, and hearing again the accents of a Voice which had haunted sixty years. 'Little children, yet a little while I am with you . . .' (John 13.33). How true it was now of the last remaining member of that party. And how well he was using those last rich years. The aged should study John. The Venerable Bede in the famous story, using his last breath to dictate the translation of the Fourth Gospel, was John's true disciple. He deserves more. Something of the scorn of Tennyson's Ulysses for those 'who store and hoard themselves', would bring back vigour and usefulness to many lives which have become too preoccupied with death.

This Christlike tenderness precedes a warning. He would have his people know that there must be no surrender. In the latter half of ch. 1 he has insisted on the reality and sinfulness of sin in special reference to those who were making light of evil. He writes, 'that they may not sin', for nothing in his message must be understood as conferring a licence to sin. He foresees, in fact, a twofold perversion, the base notion that sin is an abiding necessity which, like a physical defect, we 'must learn to live with', and against which strife is useless, or the equally base idea, that we may sin with licence, since we have Christ to cleanse us. No, no, John answers, the whole drift of my message is that we should not sin. In truth, we have forgiveness if we seek it in humble confession, but the whole effect of knowledge of God, God who is Light, should be to inspire a hatred of darkness and all that belongs to it.

## *37 : Son of Thunder

### 1 John 2.1–17

The reading is the same as that prescribed for Study 36, but some poignant autobiography haunts vs. 7 and 8. Love had not always been the burden of John's message. The writer of the letter we are reading had been self-seeking (Matt. 20. 20–28; Mark 10.35–45), fiery and passionate (Luke 9.51–56), and had earned a name which contained no gentleness (Mark 3.17). The Son of Thunder, his Master called him, and for all the love which his Lord, who, seeing deeper than others, saw the unborn years, gave to him, John was not then the figure whose gracious features are seen behind this epistle.

The key to the understanding of the paradox is autobiographical. The paramount necessity of love is an old commandment. It was the very essence of the gospel, 'the word which they had heard'. It was embodied in the very elements of the message 'from the beginning'. It was 'in him', part of every discourse and action of the Lord. It was 'in them', the fruit of the Spirit, and the most consistent lesson of experience. And yet, says John, it was a new commandment, and a touch of sadness haunts the phrase. The old apostle appears here to confess a life-long lack. In the evening of his ministry he had discovered the supremacy of love.

When did the change take place? The 'Son of Thunder' still lived at Ephesus. Irenaeus and Eusebius quote a story of the great Polycarp who sat at John's feet. The apostle once visited the public baths, and seeing the heretic Cerinthus there cried: 'Let us flee, lest the building fall, since Cerinthus the foe of the truth is in it.' This looks like the old John. When did the new man appear? Was it the exile on Patmos, and the vision of his Lord, which changed the character of his ministry? The day of withdrawal is sometimes the chosen time of God's Spirit, and the opportunity He makes or takes to teach a lesson long unlearned. Or was it the writing of the Gospel? Did that blessed urge, which sharpened thought and memory and moved his pen, bring back so gloriously those three years of fellowship that the aged man was sanctified anew?

Let us draw two lessons from this moving passage. The first is that it is never too late to learn. It is true that the arteries harden and the mind stiffens, but it is also true that the Holy Spirit is not restricted, and that the willing heart at any age can be delighted with fresh revelation. And note secondly that the fierce critic of Cerinthus lost none of his power by the change. In a new spirit of love he deals as faithfully with error and as uncompromisingly as he ever did in the fierce speech of an earlier ministry. With fallible tools the Great Builder builds His Church. But when for a season they lie docile in His hand, sharpened as He would have them, with what loveliness He builds. From the last years of John's ministry came the Fourth Gospel and the Epistles. The 'Son of Thunder' could not have written them. The Lord waited patiently for his death.

## 38 : The Antichrists

### 1 John 2.18–29

The 'antichrists', foreshadowings of a figure of evil which haunts New Testament prophecy, have marched in grisly train through the centuries, in nature, word and action the antitheses of Christ. Here they are the sectaries of whom John writes, nominal members of the Church at one time, but never really part of it.

John was not prepared to regard the purveyors of deadly heresy as the members of Christ. 'They withdrew,' he says, 'to make it plain that they were none of us.' He means that this was a deliberate demonstration on the part of those who had left the fellowship. The heretics left the Church in bitterness. They thought to build something greater, and in pursuit of a perverse design abandoned the Lord's people. Out of evil God brought good. The secessionists were seeking their own advantage. It turned out that they fulfilled a plan of God whereby the truth was protected. Falsehood declared itself and withdrew. In calm confidence that nothing could baffle the love of the Father, John abbreviates the process with a simple clause of purpose. It was all providential.

Observe v. 20. It seems clear that the Gnostics, whose dangerous teaching is never far from John's anxious thought, claimed, and perhaps practised, a special 'anointing'. A Gnostic document says, in the obscure language the heretics affected: 'We alone of all men are Christians, who complete the mystery at the third portal, and are anointed there with speechless anointing.' Probably the sectaries had adopted some of the rituals of the pagan 'mystery-religions', and were in the habit of exalting their ritual over the simplicities of John's flock. 'Fear not,' says the apostle, 'your anointing is real.'

Note that 'all' in the best manuscripts is the subject of 'know' not the object. 'You all know (the truth),' not, 'You know all things.' The RSV is correct, the AV(KJV) wrong. The former reading, designed by John as a riposte against the self-styled 'enlightened', is a rebuke to sacerdotalism. We are all 'priests of God', equally open to the Spirit's insight.

The next verse underlines this fact. John's approach is simple. He has warned his friends against antichristian falsehood, not because they lack intelligence, but because they possess the truth, and because every species of falsehood is alien to the truth. The *Cambridge Greek Testament* aptly says: 'Many of us think we can put the truth into people by screaming it into their ears. We do not suppose that they have any truth in them to which we can make appeal.'

# 39 : John's Last Word

## 1 John 4

The movement of John's theme has been likened to the windings of the river Maeander near which he lived. But like that same stream, for all its intricacy and turning on its course, it has beginning, progress, and safe exit to the sea. A little patience is sometimes needed to follow it, but no great literature ever yielded its best to the hasty and impatient reader.

The transition from v. 6 to v. 7 may seem abrupt, as if an unpleasant subject had been summarily dismissed, but the links are there for the finding. The power to love, no less than the faith which confesses Christ (**4.2**), mutually aid, and are both given by the Spirit of God. The antichristian spirit is selfish, exalts man, and divides the Church.

Such a quest was the tenor of John's ministry. Jerome's story is well known: 'Saint John the Evangelist, living in Ephesus in his extreme old age, when he was with difficulty carried into the church by his disciples, had no strength for longer exhortation, but could only say: "Little children, love one another." At length, the disciples and brethren who were there, wearied by the repetition, said: "Master, why do you always say this?" He replied in words worthy of himself; "Because it is the Lord's command and if that alone is done, it suffices".' It suffices, because God is love supremely, and only those who are partakers of the divine nature by faith can truly love.

In v. 8 John makes the third of his great pronouncements about God. 'God is spirit' (John **4.24**); 'God is light' (**1.5**), and now, 'God is love'. Of the three great truths the last is chief. It shows the Spirit to be personal, and it fills His glory with a warmth and life which brings it near to the heart of man. The idea has conquered the world, and even coloured some non-Christian thinking. The savagery, the terror, the cruelty of pagan theologies, have been banished. Indeed, a subtlety of temptation today lies in the attitude which presumes on the love of God and forgets God's justice and stern condemnation of sin. Fitzgerald's Omar touches the note in a quatrain from his vision of the Potter's Shop: The Pots speak and:

> *Said one—'Folks of a surly Tapster tell*
> *And daub his Visage with the smoke of Hell;*
> *They talk of some strict Testing of us—Pish!*
> *He's a Good Fellow and 'twill all be well.'*

All of which is far removed from the mighty truth of John's immortal sentence. The love of God is the love of Christ, and when that is said all is said.

## 40 : John's Faith

### 1 John 5

In the fourth verse John sums up his Apocalypse, which we shall soon read. 'Faith is the victory'. The word *pistis*, which is the commonest word in Greek for faith, occurs nowhere else in the Epistles and Gospel of John, in spite of the pervasive presence of the idea. In its Classical Greek form the word for victory, curiously enough, occurs nowhere else in the New Testament. But it is not such peculiarities of vocabulary that make the wonder of the verse. It is the profundity of the thought that faith is victory. Once faith is born in the Christian's heart, he becomes forthwith invincible. If a man grasps with full confidence the truth of v. 5, that the living God burst into human history in Christ, and in Christ wrought his salvation, nothing can destroy him.

*Like the vase, in which roses have once been distilled,*
*You may break, you may shatter the vase, if you will,*
*But the scent of the roses will cling to it still.*

Consider the audacity of such a statement. An effort of the mind is required to catch the fresh strength of a saying as it first fell from lips or pen. John, the fisherman from Palestine, wrote these words at the end of the first century of the Pax Romana. Rome ruled the world in which the apostle lived, Rome the mighty conqueror, whose word was law around the circle of the Inland Sea. If victory was the prerogative of any man, it belonged to the prince by the Tiber, whose legions were thrusting north through the lakes of Cumberland, manning the banks of the Rhine and the Danube, and holding the fierce Parthians behind the Armenian mountains. Rome was supreme.

But Rome was doomed. Already in the cryptic language of the strange book he had sent from Patmos, John had told of her defeat, and how the victory was theirs in whom Christ dwelt, who, out-living and out-dying their persecutors, were to aid in the fulfilment and fruition of the plans of the living God. Faith, 'the title-deeds of things hoped for and the evidence of things not seen' (Heb. 11.1) was to prove a mightier force than the swords of the legions, and all the power of the Empire.

## Questions and themes for study and discussion on Studies 31–40

1. Where in the Gospels is the family of the Lord mentioned?
2. What, in the Christian sense, is love?
3. What is the function of the pastor?
4. What echoes of the Fourth Gospel do you detect in 1 John 1?
5. What other writings in the New Testament has the problem of false teaching prompted?
6. Is sin clearly enough defined in modern preaching?
7. When does a Christian cease to be useful?
8. How should heresy be dealt with in the local church?
9. What is the wrath of God?
10. In what sense is faith the victory?

# THE LAST THINGS

## Resurrection and Glorification

### Introduction

Popular Christian idiom often speaks of salvation in terms of going to heaven when the believer dies. Many of our beloved hymns embody the theology of entrance into the fullness of salvation at death.

*There's a land beyond the river, that we call the sweet forever.*
*And we only reach that shore by faith's decree.*
*One by one we reach the portals, there to dwell with the immortals,*
*When they ring those golden bells for you and me.*

It is true that the New Testament sheds a little light on the intermediate state for the believer. Jesus promised the repentant thief that they would enter Paradise together on that very day (Luke 23.43). Twice Paul affirms that death—departure from the body—means to be present with the Lord (2 Cor. 5.8; Phil. 1.23). However, this state of blessedness is not the final goal of salvation. We do not depart to 'dwell with the immortals'. Our goal is rather the resurrection of the body. In biblical theology, the body is not merely an outward shell housing the real man—his soul or spirit. Such thought is found in Greek philosophy; but it is not biblical. In the Bible, the body is essential to my humanity. My body is part of myself. When a man becomes a Christian, his very body becomes a temple of the Holy Spirit (1 Cor. 6.19). God is to be glorified in the way the Christian uses his body (1 Cor. 6.20). The bodies of men as well as their souls or spirits are destined to be saved by transformation in the resurrection. Therefore the resurrection of the dead is the goal of the believer's hope.

## 41 : Life Today and Tomorrow

### John 5.19–29

One of the central doctrinal themes of the Gospel of John is eternal life. The purpose of Jesus' coming in the flesh (John

**1.**14) was that men might have eternal life by faith in Him (John **3.**16). The Authorized Version (KJV) sometimes renders this phrase 'everlasting life' as well as 'eternal life'. However, the phrase really means 'the life of the Age to Come' when the Kingdom of God will be established on the earth. This is made very clear in Jesus' conversation with the rich young ruler who asked Him what he must do to inherit eternal life (Mark **10.**17). Undoubtedly the young man was thinking of the promise in Dan. **12.**2, where the righteous are resurrected into eternal life. To inherit eternal life is equivalent to entering the Kingdom of God (Mark **10.**23), to being saved (Mark **10.**26); it is the life of the Age to Come (Mark **10.**30).

Our chapter today illustrates further how eternal life belongs to the Age to Come. 'The hour is coming when all *who are in the tombs* will hear his voice' (John **5.**28) and will be raised from their graves. Resurrection is one of the great events which stand between this age of weakness and mortality, and the Age to Come when God's people will receive the fullness of the blessings of the divine reign. 'Those who have done good' will experience the resurrection of life, and will enter the Kingdom of God. 'Those who have done evil' will be raised from the grave, but they will face the judgement of God for their evil deeds instead of eternal life. Eternal life includes the resurrection of the body; and life in the Age to Come in the Kingdom of God means resurrection life in immortal bodies.

However, since the Son of God, who is the embodiment of this life (John **14.**6), has come among men, He gives to them the gift of eternal life while they still reside in their mortal bodies. This is affirmed in v. 25: 'The hour is coming, *and now is*, when the dead will hear the voice of the Son of God, and those who hear will live.' In this verse, 'the dead' are not in the tombs—physically dead. Rather, they are the spiritually dead; and the life into which they enter is spiritual life. Although their bodies remain mortal and will finally die, their spirits are made alive (Rom **8.**10). To be alive in the spirit means to experience the life-giving work of the Holy Spirit within one's own spirit so that one enters into a living relationship with God through Jesus Christ (John **17.**3). Another way of describing this new life is that of the new birth (John **3.**3, 5). Paul describes the same experience in terms of being raised up with Christ (Eph. **2.**5, 6). It is those who have already experienced eternal life in their spirits who will experience the eternal life of the resurrection.

## 42 : Living Bread

### John 6.35–59

One of our Lord's best-known miracles is the feeding of the five thousand (John 6.4–14). Jesus took five loaves of bread and two fish, and after giving thanks, He fed the entire company from this lad's lunch.

Jesus used this as the occasion to teach the real reason for His coming among men. He did not come to provide men with enough physical bread to sustain bodily life, for, like Israel in the wilderness who were supplied with manna, to eat only physical bread will satisfy only the body and not solve the problem of death (49). Rather, Jesus is the living bread—the spiritual bread—which has come from heaven to provide men with a food which will enable them to live for ever (51). Jesus Himself is 'the true bread from heaven' (32), 'the bread of God' (33), 'the bread of life' (35), 'the living bread' (51). Jesus uses the common experience of eating and drinking food and drink to sustain bodily life as a metaphor for the spiritual act of receiving His life by spiritually eating and drinking His flesh and blood. Some interpreters have seen a reference to the Lord's Supper; His flesh is the Eucharistic bread and His blood the Eucharistic cup. However, this is not at all clear. Jesus used the same kind of metaphor of thirsting and drinking in John 4.14; 'whoever drinks of the water that I shall give him will never thirst'. His 'flesh' is not the Eucharistic bread; it is His own life which must be given sacrificially for men to receive eternal life (51). In vs. 50f., Jesus contrasts literal eating with spiritual participation. To eat Jesus' flesh and drink His blood is a vivid metaphor for participating in the eternal life He came to bring men. This is received by believing in Him (40, 47); it is the same as spiritually abiding in Him (56).

Again in this passage, as in John 5, eternal life is both present and future. 'He who believes *has* eternal life' (47). 'He who eats my flesh and drinks my blood has eternal life' (54). However, the present possession of eternal life is not the whole story. Whoever believes in Him has eternal life; and therefore, 'I will raise him up at the last day' (40). This is a refrain which resounds throughout the chapter (39, 40, 44, 54). This gives the meaning of 'living for ever' (51). To believe in Jesus means to receive His life in the spiritual realm here and now, and it will mean resurrection unto eternal life at the last day.

# 43 : 'I am the Resurrection'

## John 11.1–27

While Jesus was the incarnate Word of God, He was also a human being who knew the full range of human emotions and affections. This is why it is not surprising to read that Jesus loved Mary, Martha and Lazarus. This means that He felt a particularly warm human affection for these three friends. All of us have the experience of feeling closer to a few personal intimates than we do to our larger circle of acquaintances. These three lived in Bethany, a small town about two miles from Jerusalem. This was a home which Jesus loved to visit (Luke 10.38–42). Although the Gospels do not say so, we must assume that Jesus found refreshment in the home of His friends quite frequently (see Matt. 21.17).

It is therefore surprising to read that when Jesus heard that Lazarus was sick, He did not rush at once to the side of one of His dearest friends. Instead, He stayed two days longer where He was. He did this, however, because He knew what He was going to do. Lazarus' sickness was not finally to issue in his death (4), but would provide an occasion for Jesus to display the glory of God.

When Jesus declares His purpose to return to Judea where Bethany was located, His disciples remind Him that His life was in danger in Jerusalem. Jesus replies in parabolic words (9f.) to the effect that He has only a limited time to do His Father's work. So long as He is fulfilling His mission (walking in the day) no evil can turn Him aside. Jesus then declares that Lazarus has died, but that his death will be an occasion for strengthening the disciples' faith (15).

Jesus arrived at Bethany four days after Lazarus' death; in ancient Palestine, burial was carried out on the same day as death. Decomposition had already begun (39). Jesus assures Martha that Lazarus would rise again (23). Martha assumes that Jesus is referring to the resurrection at the end of the age, taught in Dan. 12.2, and believed by many Jews. Jesus replied in words which have comforted multitudes of sorrowers: 'I am the resurrection and the life' (25). Resurrection and the life of the Age to Come is no longer merely a hope for the future. It has invaded human experience in the incarnate Son of God. Therefore men may have a new experience of eternal life. The believer in Jesus may die physically, but death has lost its grip; he will certainly come to life again, because he already possesses eternal life; and the one who has received eternal life must live for ever. This marvellous affirmation is apparently more than Martha can grasp; so she replies by declaring her confidence in Jesus as the Messiah, the Son of God, in whom the promises of God are to be fulfilled.

## 44 : The Conqueror of Death

### John 11.28–44

The story told in this passage needs little comment. Only one word of explanation is needed. The custom of preparing a dead body for burial was very different from modern ways. The body was wrapped in a linen shroud which enveloped it completely. The feet would be bound at the ankles and the arms secured to the body with linen bandages. The face was wrapped in another cloth to keep the jaw in place. The body was then often placed in a cave-like tomb. When Jesus summoned Lazarus to come out, Lazarus, awakened from the sleep of death, struggled out of the tomb. The people apparently stood by in amazement; and Jesus had to command them to unbind Lazarus from his grave clothes.

One of the most beautiful words in the Bible is the brief statement, 'Jesus wept' (35). Although He knew what He was about to do, and that Lazarus was about to be restored to his sisters, the sight and the sounds of Mary's and Martha's grief touched Jesus to the heart, and He shared their grief, mingling His tears with theirs. All of us have had the experience at one time or another of witnessing a friend or loved one in deep sorrow. At such moments, there is little one can say or do that can assuage grief. But the realization that there are those who care so much that they enter into our grief to share it is a source of great comfort. Such is our Lord. Although the Prince of life and the Conqueror of death, He has shared our deepest humanity so that in the hour of sorrow or loss, He feels for us and shares our sorrow.

The relevance of this passage for the belief in resurrection is obvious. Resurrection of the dead is not merely an object of hope; it is a present reality, because the Conqueror of death has come among men. The resurrection of Lazarus is concrete evidence establishing Jesus' claim to be the resurrection and the life.

In one aspect, the resurrection of Lazarus was different from the resurrection which will occur at the end of the age. The eschatological resurrection will be resurrection to *eternal life* in the Age to Come. While it will be a bodily resurrection, it will be a different kind of body; one which cannot decay or die. There is no hint that Lazarus experienced this kind of resurrection. He was brought back to mortal, physical existence. He could never say, as Jesus could, 'I am the resurrection and the life.' Nevertheless, the resurrection of Lazarus is concrete evidence that Jesus was the Lord of life and the Conqueror of death.

## 45 : 'If Christ be not raised . . .'

### 1 Corinthians 15.1–26

The fifteenth chapter of 1 Corinthians is the most thorough discussion of the resurrection in the New Testament. Paul penned these words to meet a twofold problem in Corinth. The church there was a mixed congregation, made up of both Jews and Greeks. The belief in resurrection at the last day was widespread among Jews, but their tendency was to believe that the resurrection body was the restoration of the very body which had died to its former condition. On the other hand, Greeks often could not believe in the resurrection of the body. The soul or spirit belonged to the spiritual realm, the body to the physical. The physical was a hindrance to the spiritual; and 'salvation' often meant the flight of the soul at death to a blessed immortality. Paul has two major affirmations: resurrection will be *bodily* resurrection, but with a transformed body.

He begins by affirming the *fact* of Jesus' resurrection, and calls upon witnesses to the resurrected Christ. The most striking is the appearance to five hundred brethren at one time, most of whom were alive when Paul wrote. This is an appearance not recorded in the Gospels.

Paul then affirms the inseparable relationship between Jesus' resurrection and the resurrection of men. Indeed, he goes on to say that the whole Christian faith hangs upon the fact of Jesus' resurrection. If Jesus is dead, His claim to be Messiah and Son of God is falsified; His death is meaningless; 'faith is futile and you are still in your sins' (17). All knowledge of the afterlife is dependent upon Jesus' resurrection.

However, Jesus has been raised, and His resurrection is the 'first fruits' of the dead. First fruits is the actual beginning of the harvest. It is not promise or hope; it is the actual beginning of the harvest itself. This means that in Jesus, the eschatological resurrection has actually begun. An event which belongs at the end of the age has occurred in the midst of history. *The resurrection* of the dead occurs in at least two stages; Jesus' resurrection, then the resurrection of those who belong to Him. Theologically, these are not two events, although they are separated in time; they are two parts of a single event. The believer is sure of the resurrection at the last day, for in Jesus, this resurrection has already begun. Therefore, the final destruction of death (25f.) is an absolute certainty.

Resurrection in Christ is as certain as death in Adam. There are, in fact, two families of men; those in Adam, those in Christ. As all who are in Adam share Adam's death, so all who are in Christ share His life. Adam is the fountain-head of death, Christ of life (22).

# 46 : The Resurrection Body

## 1 Corinthians 15.35–58

Having established the certainty of bodily resurrection, Paul now turns to the question of the nature of the resurrection body. He first affirms that the resurrection body will be different from the mortal body, as the wheat is different from the seed from which it grows. However, the difference is not complete: it will be a real *body*. 'God gives it a body as he has chosen' (38). This is supported by the added fact that there are different kinds of bodies in the inanimate world.

Then Paul writes the only descriptive statement about the resurrection body to be found in the Bible (42–44). The physical body is perishable, dishonoured and weak. The resurrection body will be imperishable, glorious and powerful. Paul calls it a 'spiritual' body (44). This means that it will be a real body, but one which is adapted to the spiritual realm in the Age to Come. That it is a 'spiritual' body means that it has been transformed by the Holy Spirit. It is important to note that Paul says nothing about the substance of the body, except that it will be of different substance from the physical body. It will be of such a substance that it cannot know decay, humiliation or weakness. It is a body such as we cannot now conceive. 'Flesh and blood', i.e. our present, mortal, physical bodies, 'cannot inherit the kingdom of God' (50). In their glorified resurrected bodies, made like to the glorious resurrection body of Christ (48f.), the saints will enter the Kingdom of God to dwell with God for ever.

Paul concludes with a brief affirmation of the eschatological resurrection. Not all the saints will have fallen asleep in death; but those who are alive will experience the same change as the dead saints (51). The trumpet which is to sound is probably the same trumpet mentioned in 1 Thess. 4.16 (see Matt. 24.31). Both the living and the dead saints will be instantaneously transformed by exchanging their mortal, perishable bodies for immortal, imperishable ones. This will mean the abolition of death. Death will be swallowed up in victory. 'The last enemy to be destroyed is death' (26). Thus the saints will enter the blessing of the eternal Kingdom of God.

## Questions and themes for study and discussion on Studies 41–46

1. Do we really need to know anything about the intermediate state other than that we will be with the Lord?
2. Think of what it means to glorify God in my earthly body. Be specific.
3. Is the immortality of the human soul taught in Scripture? See 1 Tim. 6.16.
4. Was Lazarus raised to eternal life or returned to earthly life? What is the difference between Lazarus' resurrection and Jesus' resurrection?
5. Did Jesus experience the full range of human emotions (John 11.35)? Does He understand *your* feelings?
6. Can one not have a meaningful faith in God apart from belief in the resurrection (1 Cor. 15.17)?

# CHARACTER STUDIES

## *47 : John's Exile

### Revelation 1.1–9; 4.1–6

We return a little down the years to an earlier time in John's ministry. He was a prisoner on Patmos. It was probably during the time when Domitian, that execrable creature who ruled Rome in the eighties of the first century, was putting pressure on the authorities in Ephesus to persecute the Church.

It may actually have been for the safety of an aged and respected member of the city that John was sent across to Patmos. The Romans called such removal 'relegation', and, if the guess is correct, the old bishop would enjoy the freedom of the island, provided he abstained from subversive activities. There is no evidence that he was under harsh duress in a labour camp. At any rate he kept in touch with the churches of his 'diocese', and wrote letters to them carefully couched in allusive, poetic language, which only the recipients would understand. His whole book, written perhaps on some vantage point, is interwoven with poetic imagery based on the island's common scenery, as every visitor to Patmos realizes. As the sun slopes, all the sea to the west can be awash with gold (4.6), as John saw it when he pictured the saints beside a glassy sea. The sea in fact, filled his mind. Its sounds are everywhere, as they are all through the Greek islands of the Aegean. Christ's voice was for the writer 'like the sound of many waters' (1.15), something universal heard everywhere, speaking over and through all other sounds.

And sometimes the mood might change. The sea, like the moving mass of mankind, is capricious, cruel. John saw 'a beast rise out of the sea', with a name of blasphemy on his head.

This, in his first meaning, was Rome and her Emperor, who demanded worship from men as a test of loyalty. Perhaps John had looked down on the land-locked harbour between the hills, which almost cuts the island in half. Perhaps he had seen some great galley of Rome loom over the horizon and come in under heavy sail, or with her three banks of oars flashing.

He might have looked east and discerned low down the pale blue coast of Asia where his beloved people endured the stress of persecution. It bore heavily and hard upon the folk of Smyrna, the ruins of whose town lie somewhere deep below the streets of modern Izmir. The old leader would have gladly stood by the persecuted community, but the sea lay wide and decisively between him and them.

In his poem he pictured, as many yearning souls have pictured, a happier age, a quieter and more gentle world. 'And there shall be no more sea' (21.1), he wrote, no more cruel separation, no forced parting, no gulf fixed between men and women who should be together. The phrase becomes poignant in its context.

## *48 : Christ in Glory

### Revelation 1.10–20

It seems almost too audacious to set this flashing vision of the glorified Christ among the characters of Scripture, but in the context of this book's poetry it must be done. Some of the symbolism is not clear to us because much apocalyptic literature is lost. Though not biblical, it provided a store of symbols. For example, the rabbis seem to have used *aleph* and *tau*, the A and Z of the Hebrew alphabet, just as the first and last letters of the Greek alphabet are here used, to express comprehensiveness, and all-embracing communication. God has said all He has to say in Christ. He comprehends all history and remains God's last word to man. And consider the golden lampstands. If John wrote during Domitian's persecution, after A.D. 81, the seven-branched candlestick had already lain with the Jewish loot in Rome's Temple of Peace for over a decade. But in Zechariah's day, six centuries before, the lovely piece of furniture was already a symbol (Zech. 4). The seven churches uphold the light of God's presence, but are inseparable from a central Christ (13). We know of churches at Troas, Hierapolis and Colossae, all in Asia, so why John chose the particular seven is not clear, save that the sacred number was a symbol for perfection.

This does not exhaust the echoes of the chapter, and it is not intended here to do so, but consider the audacity of faith which saw all the future, not in Caesar, but in the blameless Galilean who had died in Jerusalem, and had risen again. Only the stark fact of that triumph over death could explain a confidence so superb. The writer was suffering for his faith.

And bear in mind that the one who could write down the blazing imagery of this divine person, struggling like Ezekiel in his opening chapter to catch the transcendental in human speech, had known the Son of Man. He had also seen Him gasp away His life upon the cross, and in the murk of dawn had raced to the tomb to find it empty. That was half a toilsome century before. What utter conviction of faith invincible was this!

## 49 : The Ephesians

### Revelation 2.1–7; Acts 20.17–35

We have met the Ephesians before in this series. In fact we know them better than most of the congregations of the early Church. They had been well-taught by Paul, Timothy and John, and could recognize impostors, and stand firm against those who sought to soften their loyalty. They belonged to an ancient city. Ephesus was already ten centuries old when Paul hired the school of Tyrannus in which to preach. It was a fine city. To stand today on the marble street and look along its length to the great curve of the theatre set in the side of the hill, is to gain a deep impression of the wealth and ability of those who built and adorned the city of Artemis.

The little group who followed Christ in the pagan capital of Asia had much to contend with. The temple of Artemis drew pilgrims and tourists from the whole world, and we have seen how sensitive entrenched heathendom and its commercialized religion was to any assault from dissident groups. Ephesus was dependent upon the industries which flowed from the worship of the goddess, and the violent and scornful proletariat was not tolerant of the church. Hence the strength of the liberal movement of the Nicolaitans, who sought to ease the confrontation.

Ephesus held some of the weariness of an ancient community. The great thesis of Sir William Ramsay was that the spirit of a community finds, for good and ill, a subtle expression in the tone and outlook of the Christian community in its midst. He showed how a deep understanding of the seven churches of these two chapters, gave some idea of the reasons for their faults and excellencies. And the Ephesian congregation showed some marks of the venerable city in which it lived. It had grown a little battle-weary, and the valiant old man on Patmos feared that they might not continue to fight on.

A new infusion of life was needed. There are coins of Ephesus which show a date-palm, a tree sacred to Artemis, as a symbol of her gift of life and fruitfulness. To those prepared to strive, John promised: 'I will give him to eat of the tree of life.' A generation later according to Ignatius, the Ephesians were running well. As late as A.D. 431 a notable episcopal council was held there. But the decline set in. The harbour filled with silt. The Turks came with blight and ruin. The candlestick fell.

## 50 : The Smyrnaeans

### Revelation 2.8–11; John 16.1–4

Persecution was falling heavily on Smyrna, and the enduring church needed their leader's word. Youthful Smyrna was Ephesus' rival, and to Smyrna's brave church was promised a 'crown of life'. The Christians of Smyrna would fasten on the words with satisfaction, for it was the sort of poet's tag on which cities preen themselves. Athens was 'violet-crowned', until men tired of Pindar's adjective. Of Auckland, where these words are written, to its citizens' delight, Kipling wrote, 'last, loneliest, loveliest, exquisite, apart'. In such fashion the simile of a crown dominates all praise of Smyrna. Aristides calls the 'Golden Street', which ringed Mount Pagus with lovely buildings, 'the crown of Ariadne in the heavenly constellation'. Apollonius of Tyana, amid praise for Smyrna, says rhetorically that it is greater charm 'to wear a crown of men than a crown of porticoes'.

'I have been there,' wrote Freya Stark, of Mount Pagus' crest, 'sometimes to walk in the morning, with Ionia on one side and Aeolis on the other, spread below; and nearby, in a shapeless depression, the stadium where Polycarp was burned, and have thought of that old bishop, how he would describe his intercourse with John, and with the rest of those who had seen the Lord . . .' Under 'the crown of Smyrna', Polycarp was not the only Christian who won 'a crown of life'.

Polycarp was born perhaps in A.D. 64, and suffered martyrdom in 155, in a persecution in which Jews joined the pagans. He claimed to have served Christ all his ninety years of life. Polycarp forms a link between the Apostolic age and the end of the second century, when those whom he taught were still active.

Smyrna, which still lives as the vigorous port of Izmir, won from John unstinted admiration. Its congregation was the salt of Asia. The church, purged by suffering, continued to stand through succeeding centuries. Smyrna was among the last cities to be submerged by Islam, and it was such delaying actions in the East which allowed the West time to arise from the torpor of the Dark Ages. Fidelity is fruitful beyond its own generation. For the menaced and the persecuted, the Resurrection, real, historical, factual, was and is an enduring anchor of the soul.

# 51 : The Pergamenes

## Revelation 2.12–17; 20.10–15

Pergamum, royally situated, round a great acropolis, with a view of far ranges, the sea, and the purple peaks of Lesbos, had been a seat of government for four hundred years. It was a capital city in pre-Roman days, and when the last of her kings, seeing the shape of emerging history, bequeathed his kingdom to the Romans in 133 B.C., Pergamum became the chief town of the new province of Asia. It was natural that the first temple of the imperial cult—that worship of the emperor on which the Christians looked with deep abhorrence—should be located here. A temple to Rome and Augustus was erected in Pergamum in 29 B.C., and thus 'the worship of the Beast' came to Asia. But other cults beside that of Rome were endemic. There was the worship of Asklepios, the god of healing, whose symbol was a serpent coiled round a bending sapling. The emperor raises his right hand in the exact gesture of the Nazi salute.

The letter is addressed to those who dwell 'where Satan's throne is', and Christians must have found something peculiarly satanic in the town's pre-occupation with the serpent image. Pausanias, the Greek traveller, who wrote many descriptions of ancient cities, spoke of Asklepios as 'sitting on a throne with a staff in his hand, and his other hand upon the head of a serpent'. The church in Pergamum found the surrounding symbolism of paganism quite diabolical. There was also the magnificent throne-like altar to Zeus, which stood royally on the crag dominating the city, and which is now in the East Berlin Museum. The altar commemorated the defeat of a Gallic invasion of Asia, under the imagery of the legendary struggle between the gods and goddesses of Olympus and the giants. The giants, in accordance with Pergamum's prevailing obsession, are represented as a brood of Titans, with snake-like tails. Zeus, to whom the throne-like altar was dedicated, was called 'Zeus the Saviour', and the title would impress Christian minds as blasphemous.

They must have called the great altar 'Satan's throne', and so put the phrase in the Apocalpyse. It helped embattled Christians, under the shadow of arrogant paganism and facing a hostile world, to know that One remembered 'where they lived'. It helps still.

## 52 : Jezebel of Thyatira

### Revelation 2.18–29

In the letter to Thyatira, under another figure of speech from the Old Testament, the Nicolaitans appear again. Thyatira was a centre of commerce. More trade guilds have left traces at Thyatira than those of any other Asian city. Inscriptions mention wool-workers, linen-workers, dyers, leather-workers, tanners, potters, bakers, slave-dealers, and bronzesmiths. The dyers have left one mark which suggests the geographical breadth of Thyatiran trade. They brewed a red dye, probably the modern Turkey-red, from the madder root, which grows abundantly in the district. The ancient purple was a colour nearer scarlet than blue, and it was this dye that the business-woman, Lydia, was selling 500 miles away in Philippi in A.D. 52. In that year Paul arrived and found 'a certain woman named Lydia, a seller of purple from the city of Thyatira' (Acts 16.14).

Whether Lydia still lived when John wrote is not known. It is odd that two women of Thyatira should appear in the New Testament, one the gracious hostess of Paul, the other, 'Jezebel', the target of another apostle's scorn.

Jezebel, Ahab's consort, was the seal of a trade alliance with Phoenicia, and there is no doubt that Ahab's Israel derived immense wealth from business conducted with the busy heathen on the coast. The oil and wheat of Israel went down to Tyre (Ezek. 27). The wealth of the world flowed back. Ahab was rich. He built an ivory house in Samaria, the foundations and the broad steps of which can still be seen. But prosperity is not always good for a nation. With Tyrian goods came Tyrian gods. With Jezebel came Baal. It is possible, therefore, that the choice on Carmel involved more than theology. When the people chose Yahweh they precipitated an economic depression. A break with Jezebel was a break with Tyre.

The woman in Thyatira, a clever woman with a gift of speech who professed to interpret God's will, offered, as Jezebel did, prosperity at the price of compromise. As a Nicolaitan, she believed in establishing a compromise with society. In Thyatira, in fact, it must have been commercial ruin not to do so. Anxious men must have longed for some formula of conduct by which they could maintain both their livelihood, so dependent upon their membership of the guild, and their allegiance to Christ. Was the hard choice Christ or poverty? 'No,' said Jezebel. 'Keep your heart intact. Learn "the deep things" of religion, and you will see that even behind pagan worship lives an acknowledgement of the Most High God. Go to the sacrifice but think there of Christ. Attend the feasts, but set an example of purity and moderation.' 'Look,' answers John, 'I set her on a dining couch, and her vile associates with her, and they shall have opportunity to enjoy—great tribulation, unless *they* repent, for she has shown that *she* cannot repent.'

## 53 : The Lesson of the Nicolaitans

### 2 Corinthians 6

The solemn lesson to be learned from the compromising group which we have followed for some distance, from Corinth to Thyatira requires a last word. These 'characters of the New Testament' fall under fierce condemnation. And yet how strong was the temptation to confront a hostile world less harshly. It still is, and it is only unbalanced characters who actually enjoy unpopularity and persecution.

Was John, then, too harsh? Sir William Ramsay answers the question well. 'The historian,' he writes, 'must regard the Nicolaitans with intense interest, and must deeply regret that we know so little about them ... And yet at the same time he must feel that nothing could have saved the infant Church from melting away into one of those vague and ineffective schools of philosophic ethics except the stern and strict rule laid down by John. An easy-going Christianity could never have survived; it could not have conquered the world; only the most convinced, resolute adherence to the most uncompromising interpretation of its own principles could have given the Christians the courage and self-reliance that were needed. For them to hesitate or to doubt was to be lost.'

The cost was heavy—in loss, in physical and mental suffering. In Nero's Rome, unpopularity begat persecution. Ephesus revealed a reaction as savage. In Bithynia, State repression followed the hostile protest of resentful paganism. In these studies we have traced the first attempts of Christians to live at peace with paganism; we have read the warnings of Paul, and seen how, in disregard of those warnings, a group emerged who abused the noble doctrine of liberty and mingled Christ determinedly with Belial. As the New Testament closes, the long years of State persecution had opened. They were to cleanse and purify the Church. But the Church could never have survived the impact of those years had there not been in her midst a body of men and women who literally 'counted all things but loss for Christ'. We bow the head before those who bore all the human heart finds it most difficult to bear, to preserve the faith unsullied, unadulterated, undamaged and intact.

Professor Butterfield's words still stand: 'We are back for the first time in the earliest centuries of Christianity, and those centuries afford some relevant clues to the kind of attitude to adopt.'

## Questions and themes for study and discussion on Studies 47–53

1. How did John turn misfortune to advantage?
2. Need one interpretation of a prophecy exclude another?
3. How does a church grow weary?
4. How does a church grow strong?
5. The Church and 'Satan's Seat' today.
6. How does surrounding society get into the Church?
7. Today's Nicolaitans.

# THE LAST THINGS

## Judgement in the Teaching of Jesus

### Introduction

The Bible pictures God as filling many roles in His relationship to men. He is the Eternal King ruling His people; He is the Good Shepherd caring for His flock; He is the Heavenly Father who provides for His family; He is also the Law-giver and the Judge of men.

In the Bible, ethics is always theologically grounded. That is to say, right and wrong are not determined by custom or convention, by the human conscience, whether individual or collective, but by the will of God. In simple language, right is right and wrong is wrong because God has decreed it. There are, therefore, standards of right and wrong which are normative and definitive, for they are rooted in the will of God. This is not to say that *all* human conduct is determined by these absolutes. Paul himself asserts the principle of expediency in certain matters (1 Cor. 10.23). However, underlying all human conduct is the bed-rock of the will of God for human conduct.

God has made man a free moral agent. He is ethically responsible for his decisions and his conduct. God does not compel him to conform to the right; he leaves it for man to choose his course of action.

God holds man responsible for his conduct. The entire Bible points to a day of judgement when men will stand face to face with God and give an account of the things done in the body. The day of judgement is spoken of both as the judgement seat of God (Rom. 14.10) and the judgement seat of Christ (2 Cor. 5.10). God in Christ will be the final judge. However, since Christ has already appeared among men, they are already faced with decision, for or against Christ. Judgement is both future and present. These ideas will be developed in the sections that follow.

## 54 : False Hopes

### Matthew 3.7-12; 5.21-26

In Old Testament times, the people of Israel were constantly disobedient to the demands of God's Law and turned again and again to worship the false gods of their neighbours. The central message of the prophets was the warning that such apostasy meant judgement. 'Prepare to meet your God, O Israel' (Amos 4.12).

In New Testament times, Israel experienced a devotion to the Law unknown in Old Testament times. The scribes were professional students and interpreters of the Law, and the Pharisees were those among the people who rigorously obeyed the scribal legislation. The Sadducees were the priestly caste who served in the Temple and carried out the innumerable animal sacrifices demanded by the Law. Outwardly, Israel looked like a faithful people, obediently fulfilling the divine decrees. However, instead of a nation humbly dependent on God, Israel had become a proud people who gloried in their obedience to the Law and boasted of their national descent.

Then came John the Baptist. He demanded repentance—a change of life style. Repentance means simply 'right-about face'. It was folly to boast of descent from Abraham. God was able from the stones to raise up children to Abraham (9). The point of this warning is that Jews of John's day claimed salvation, not because they loved God, but because they were descendants of Abraham. John ridiculed this as a false hope. He warned of the day of judgement and the appearance of one who would separate men. As the farmer threshes out the grain, burning the chaff and storing the wheat, so, said John, one will come who will separate men, submitting the wicked to judgement and bringing the righteous into His Kingdom. The important point is that this judgement will depend upon the attitude of the heart and not upon membership in the favoured nation.

Jesus in the Sermon on the Mount said essentially the same thing. A faithful Jew boasted in the fact that he kept the Law. For instance, a righteous man never violated the command against murder. Jesus replied that that is not enough. If a man nurses anger, hostility, hatred in his heart, he has failed to fulfil God's requirement. One can heap epithets of hatred—'Fool, idiot (*raca*)'—upon his brother and not formally violate the Law. Jesus said that God seeks a heart that harbours no evil toward his neighbour. Any other spirit, correct though a man may be in outward acts, will incur the divine judgement.

## 55 : A Final Separation

### Luke 17.20–31

Jesus' message about the Kingdom of God was twofold. The Kingdom of God will come at the end of the age when all evil will be swept away and God in the person of the Son of man will alone be King (Matt. **19**.28). However, this very Kingdom of God—the sovereign rule of the heavenly King—has broken into history in the person and mission of Jesus (Matt. **12**.28) and is now confronting men with its demands. Men must now receive the offer of the Kingdom of God in Jesus with all the trustfulness and humility of a child to enter the future Kingdom of God (Mark. **10**.15).

Many of the people responded to Jesus' teachings and became His disciples. His chief opponents were the Pharisees, in part because He cut through their legalism and demanded a change of heart.

One day they asked Him when the Kingdom of God was coming. Their question was directed to the future coming of the Kingdom which they believed would crush evil and vindicate Israel—and them—as the people of God. Jesus replied that the Kingdom was already in their midst, but in an unexpected form; it was not accompanied by the signs and outward display the Pharisees expected, and without which they were not satisfied.

Then Jesus gave His disciples the instruction in the coming of the Kingdom, which He had refused to the Pharisees. The Son of man will come in power and glory. His coming will be as sudden and visible as a flash of lightning streaking across the sky. However, before His coming in glory, He has come in humility to suffer and die. When He comes in glory, men will be so completely engrossed in ordinary human activities that they will be overtaken suddenly and unexpectedly. The reference to the days of Noah and of Lot is not to the evil and wickedness of these times, but to complete neglect of the things of God. That day will not come as a surprise to those who are ready for it. Those who love the Lord and serve God—those who have accepted the offer of the Kingdom in Jesus' person—will be ready to welcome the King whenever He comes.

# 56 : A People Under Judgement

## Luke 20.1-19, 45-47

Toward the end of Jesus' ministry, His opponents, the scribes and Pharisees, and the priests and Sadducees, frequently engaged Him in debate, trying to trap Him. This question about Jesus' authority was such a question. Authority was one of the most characteristic features of Jesus' teaching. Early, He brought about the reaction, 'What is this? A new teaching! With authority he commands even the unclean spirits, and they obey him' (Mark 1.27). The Jews did not really want an answer to their questions; they hoped only to trap Jesus. He answered them by turning the question back upon them, thus outwitting them.

Then He told them a parable about a vineyard and its wicked tenants. This story is true to life in that there were large farms around Galilee owned by absentee landlords and leased out to tenants. The evil tenants represent Israel and her leaders. God had sent a succession of prophets to them, whom they had rejected. Then He sent His Son—Jesus—and the tenants plotted His death. Even as the landlord would punish the evil tenants, so God will bring His judgement upon Israel, 'and give the vineyard to others' (16).

This parable marks a turning point in redemptive history. The people of Israel were 'the sons of the kingdom' (Matt. 8.12) in that they were the sons of Abraham, the recipients of God's promises, the keepers of God's Law, and the natural heirs of the Kingdom of God. This is why Jesus limited His mission largely to the Jewish people (Matt. 10.5f.). However, when Israel rejected Jesus' offer, they disqualified themselves as the sons of the Kingdom. Henceforth, the sons of the Kingdom would be those who received Jesus' offer of the Kingdom (Matt. 13.38). Matthew's account of this parable adds this verse: 'Therefore I tell you, the kingdom of God will be taken away from you and given to a nation producing the fruits of it' (Matt. 21.43). This was a judgement which was fulfilled in history. In A.D. 70, Roman armies completely destroyed Jerusalem, and not long afterwards the Jewish nation was dispersed from their homeland. Israel ceased to be the custodian of the Kingdom of God; her place has been taken by the Church, a holy 'nation' (1 Pet. 2.9).

The last three verses in today's text illustrate one of the reasons why Israel's leaders were rejected by our Lord. They loved the prestige and honour that accompanied their position of leadership, but were little concerned with human need and distress. They were more devoted to the preservation and exaltation of forms and traditions than they were to alleviating human need. Elsewhere, Jesus said of them, 'woe to you, scribes and Pharisees, hypocrites! for you tithe mint and dill and cummin (the smallest of shrubs), and have neglected the weightier matters of the law, justice and mercy and faith' (Matt. 23.23).

# 57 : 'Watch'

## Matthew 25

In His Olivet Discourse (Matt. 24), Jesus outlined the course of the age, and the main events which will occur at the end of the age—the coming of Antichrist, the Great Tribulation, and the Parousia of the Son of man. To this discourse Matthew adds three parables which have a single purpose: to warn His disciples to 'watch' in view of the unknown hour of the end. 'Watch therefore, for you do not know on what day your Lord is coming' (Matt. 24.42, 43; 25.13). The Greek word translated 'watch' does not mean to watch for something, but simply to be awake.

Men must be awake to their own spiritual condition if the return of the Lord is not to catch them unawares. This is illustrated by the parable of the ten bridesmaids. All were invited to the wedding, all were dressed properly, all carried lamps, as the custom was, to join in the wedding procession. However, only five had lighted lamps; five did not have a supply of oil. This symbolizes proper church membership and formally correct Christian profession without a genuine Christian experience. As Jesus said, men must be born from above of the Holy Spirit to enter the Kingdom of God (John 3.3–5).

Men must be awake to their opportunities to serve their Master if His coming is not to take them by surprise. A 'talent' was worth about four hundred pounds or a thousand dollars—a very substantial sum of money. The man who had only two talents received the same commendation as the man who had five talents, for the basis of reward is not actual achievement but faithfulness of devotion. The man with one talent had an equal opportunity, but he was a 'do-nothing' Christian, and he received no reward. If the parable is pressed in details, it might seem to teach that he lost his salvation. However, a parable cannot be pressed in all its details. The point is: How can any man who professes that he had received the incomparable salvation Christ freely offers be unwilling to devote himself in faithful service to his Lord? Such a man is a contradiction in terms.

The third parable has been diversely interpreted. The key question is, who are Jesus' 'brethren' (40)? If, as some say, they are all human beings in need, this parable teaches a salvation by works. However, Jesus once said that those who do the will of God are His brothers (Matt. 12.49f.). With this as the key to the parable, it teaches that Jesus will send His brethren—His disciples—into all the world, and in the day of judgement, the destiny of the nations of men will be determined by their response to Jesus' representatives. Some will welcome these itinerant preachers into their homes and feed them (Matt. 10.9–13); they will visit them and minister to them when they are imprisoned (Luke 21.12). 'He who receives you receives me, and he who receives me receives him who sent me' (Matt. 10.40). Those who have received Jesus' brethren and treated them well will enter into the Kingdom of God in the day of judgement; those who have rejected them and ill-treated them will be excluded from the Kingdom. The destiny of the world depends on how it responds to Jesus' disciples as they carry the good news of the gospel into all the world.


## 58 : Judged Already

### John 3.16–21, 31–36; 12.44–50

In the passage last considered—the parable of the sheep and goats—the judge was the Son of man who one day will sit as King upon His glorious judgement throne. In His incarnation and earthly ministry, the Judge was present among men, facing them with decision for or against Himself. Therefore, judgement in principle is already effected as men are confronted with the person and words of Jesus, even though the execution of that judgement awaits the coming of the last day; and the same judgement continues to be carried out as men today are confronted by the message of the gospel and brought to decision.

This fact of judgement in history is most vividly stated in John's Gospel. God sent His Son for the purpose of accomplishing the world's salvation. We have seen in our earlier readings that the eternal life which belongs to the Age to Come was present in Jesus' person and offered to men. However, they must respond affirmatively to it. Life is in Christ, and those who believe in Him —who receive Him—already *have* everlasting life. Salvation— the possession of eternal life—these are synonymous terms.

As a man decides for or against Christ, his decision determines his destiny, and in effect, the act of judgement has already taken place in his decision. 'He who believes in him is not condemned; he who does not believe is condemned already, because he has not believed in the name of the only Son of God' (18).

This theme of present judgement is reiterated in John. God has given all authority to His Son. The one who believes in Him has already entered into the experience of eternal life, and therefore has passed through the judgement and been found faithful by the Judge. But the one who does not obey the Son, whose first demand is for faith in Himself, has in his negative decision sealed his doom. He shall not see life, but rather stands under the wrath of God (36).

While God has committed all authority to Jesus, and has given to Him the prerogative of the Judge of men, we have already seen that the primary purpose of His mission is not to judge the world but to bring salvation (**12**.47b). He has come as a light into the world in order that men may not remain in darkness (**12**.46). There is a sense in which it is not Jesus Himself who judges (**12**.47). Jesus is the purveyor of the word of God; He is in fact the living embodiment of God's word (**1**.1). It is Jesus' word which judges men (**12**.48). We have a parallel to this in the Synoptics. 'For whoever is ashamed of me and *of my words* . . ., of him will the Son of man also be ashamed when he comes in the glory of his Father with the holy angels' (Mark **8**.38). In John, Jesus affirms that it will be His word that He has spoken which will judge His hearers on the last day. Jesus and His word are inseparable. His person, His work, are embodied in His word. As men receive His word, they receive Him, and as they reject the word, they reject Him. The essential judgement is made in this life as men are confronted by Jesus' word and make a decision for or against it; but this judgement will be carried out in the last day.

This last passage should remind us, as present-day disciples, of our sober responsibility. Jesus is no longer with us in physical presence, but His word is with us. We are the custodians of His word. As we confront men with the same word that He proclaimed, we challenge them with the unavoidable opportunity for decision, for or against Christ. In this sense, Christians today are the agents of judgement to those who hear Jesus' word from us. This is an exciting but also a sobering realization. We cannot regard the Christian life lightly or casually.

## Questions and themes for study and discussion on Studies 54–58

1. Is upbringing in a Christian family assurance that one will be a true Christian? Why not?
2. In the light of the value of a talent, can anyone refuse to serve God actively because he is only a 'one-talent man'?
3. The parable of the sheep and the goats is told in the idiom of the mission of Jesus' disciples as itinerant preachers. How are we to apply it to the established Church and professional ministry of today?

# CHARACTER STUDIES

## 59 : The Sardians

### Revelation 3.1–6; 18.1–8

Sardis, ancient capital of Lydia, old realm of Croesus the Rich, fell out of history. Some ruins lie round and under a great crumbling crag, the old acropolis, in the Hermus valley, and a small village called Sart is nearby. Once it was a road junction, straddling trade-routes, a mingling-place of cultures. Its crag, where temples and palaces stood, a great spur of mountain, was seemingly impregnable, dominating the surrounding country.

And yet it seems that the mighty strength of the city on the ridge bred over-confidence, and twice in history the acropolis was taken, and a war ended, by men scaling the heights, 'like thieves in the night', and storming the walls by a surprise attack. 'It was a city,' wrote Ramsay, who found the key to the character of Sardis in her history, 'whose story blazoned forth the uncertainty of human fortunes, and the shortness of the step which separates over-confident might from sudden disaster. It was a city whose name was synonymous with pretensions unjustified, promise unfulfilled, appearance without reality, confidence which heralded ruin.'

If Ramsay's thesis holds, and John's stern letter suggests as much, the city's Christians, like their community, had not used great advantages well. Preoccupied with their own affairs, they had not recognized the resourcefulness of the foe. How the majority had failed is not clear. It is a few only who had 'not defiled their garments'. Columns of a temple to Cybele stand on the valley floor, and hers was an Asiatic cult, with perverted sexualities, full of wild excitement, clashing cymbals, blaring horns and obscene mutilations. Perhaps some form of Nicolaitanism had corrupted the church with compromise in this regard. 'Defiled garments' suggests some unworthy conduct. The emperor-cult was also rife at Sardis, and the city had built a temple in honour of Tiberius at the time of the great Asian earthquake.

Those who held true were to 'walk in white', like generals in a triumph. We know no more of the Sardian church. A cross cut here and there into the stone suggests that the goddess' temple was used at one time for Christian worship, but the rest is silence.

# 60 : The Philadelphians

## Revelation 3.7–13; Matthew 28.16–20

Philadelphia, whose name means 'brotherly love', was founded
in the middle of the second century before Christ, and named by
its founder, Eumenes of Pergamum, in honour of his loyal brother
Attalus. The city was an outpost of Greek culture in Asia, but had
little history until the great earthquake of A.D. 17 brought a
catastrophe. Tacitus, the Roman historian, writes: 'The same
year twelve cities of Asia collapsed because of an earthquake
which took place at night, a calamity the more serious because
it fell without warning. Escape into open country was no help
because people were swallowed up by the gaping earth. Great
mountains crumbled to rubble, and plains were thrust up into
hills ...' Telling of Tiberius' bounteous earthquake-relief,
Tacitus lists Philadelphia.

The trouble was that there was no end to disaster. The city
was near the faultline, on the edge of a volcanic district named
'the Burntland', from the masses of scoria debris which strewed
the countryside, and seems for a long time to have been subject
to demoralizing earth tremors. Strabo, the geographer, writing
in A.D. 20 said; 'Philadelphia is full of earthquakes ... its very
walls are unreliable, but daily fall apart.' Escape to the surrounding countryside was a common experience, and many would
live for long periods in tents on the safer ground. Hence the
letter: 'I will make him a pillar in the temple of my God, and he
shall go out thence no more' (12). The Philadelphian church was
a tormented congregation, its poor homes ruined, its life in
jeopardy.

In gratitude to Tiberius the city took a new name. It called
itself Neocaesarea, but the old name reasserted itself. The
Philadelphians tried unsuccessfully to write upon themselves
'the name of their god' (12).

When Eumenes founded Philadelphia he chose a notable
situation. South-east from the Hermus Valley, a long vale runs
into the plateau of Asia Minor, a main line of communication
between Smyrna and Lydia, and Phrygia. Hence the phrase 'I
have set before thee an open door which none can shut'. Philadelphia was the keeper of the gateway to central Asia Minor, a
city conscious of its mission as a centre of Hellenism, and aware
of its frontier position. In such a city a missionary church was
natural. That role was to be strikingly illustrated in later

centuries when Rome had fallen, and Constantinople, her surviving successor, was facing the pressure of Islam, rolling in from Asia. Gibbon, in chapter 64 of his great *Decline and Fall*, almost echoes John's praise of long before. Until the exchange of minorities between Turkey and Greece in 1922, there was still a Christian witness there.

# 61 : The Laodiceans

## Revelation 3.14–22; Isaiah 1.1–18

Laodicea was no natural fortress. The low swell of ground on which its fortifications stood, could have presented no great problem for an invader, and as a strong-point Laodicea had a disastrous weakness. The water-supply came by a vulnerable aqueduct from springs six miles away to the north. A place with its water so exposed to enemy action could scarcely stand a siege. Under Rome, Laodicea grew in commercial importance. Cicero travelled that way in 51 B.C. on his way to Cilicia, and the fact that he cashed drafts in Laodicea shows that the city was already a place of financial importance. There were manufacturers too. The valley produced a glossy black wool, and the strain of sheep bred for the trade was to be traced until the nineteenth century. The wool was the basis of a textile industry.

Laodicea had a medical school. The names of its physicians early appear on coins, and there is also the device of the serpent-wreathed rod of Asklepios, the god of healing. It was probably the medical school of Laodicea which developed the Phrygian eye-powder, famous in the ancient world.

Hence the scornful imagery. The black garments exported all over the Mediterranean world, the famous eye-ointment, the city's wealth, all are there, forming a structure for the writer's reproaches.

It is possible that the letter quoted the very words of some civic inscription. In A.D. 60 a terrible earthquake 'prostrated the city'. The phrase is that of Tacitus, who wrote fifty years later. The Roman Senate again gave vast sums to devastated Asian cities, but the historian records that Laodicea refused all such aid. She rose again, writes Tacitus, 'with no help from us.' The proud fact would undoubtedly be recorded on stone.

In prosperity men too commonly decay, and the Christian community of the city had become infected with the spirit of the place. The city on an open high-road may have learned the arts of compromise in the school of history, and now she was 'neither cold nor hot'. So, too, was the church which found a place in the self-confident, easy-going community.

Whatever the cause, ease, wealth, prosperity, the pervading spirit of the place, the life of the church-community was at a low ebb. It is curious that such a state should accompany an absence of enemies or persecution. Opulence and a facile environment have not normally been the stimuli of human progress. The pressure of hard and difficult conditions has been rather the prerequisite of achievement. Physically at ease, Laodiceans had grown indifferent to the call to work and strive for excellence. They remain a warning for an age of affluence.

# 62 : The Christians of Hierapolis

## Colossians 4

Whether or not Philip ended his days in Hierapolis, churches clustered in the broad and fertile Lycus Valley. First came Colossae, and further east, six miles apart on either side of the valley plain, lay Hierapolis to the north, and Laodicea to the south. There is nothing to be seen of Laodicea, though the humped irregular ground under the fields suggest that a task awaits the archaeologists. Hierapolis, from whose locality Laodicea drew its water, was a spa, and abundant remains of market place and cemetery, suggest that it was rich and well patronized.

Paul ordered an interchange of letters between Laodicea and Colossae, and John must surely have included Hierapolis in his strictures on Laodicea, or he would not have used the illustration of the lukewarm water. To stand in the oatfields of Laodicea and look north, is to see the white cliff at Pummakale, where Hierapolis stood. The silica-laden water has spilled over from hot springs, and in a series of beautiful white natural basins, it runs to the valley below. Any New Zealander knows the geology of such a site, for the Rotorua spa demonstrates similar phenomena. The lukewarm chemical-laden water is also just such an emetic as John describes. Those who knew the place would recognize the imagery. Here in the broad, prosperous valley were affluent Christians, a sickly brew, neither sturdily Christian nor frankly pagan, and disgustingly burdened with alien admixture.

Psa. **119**.113 says, as Moffatt renders it: 'I hate men who are half and half', and it was the rugged Elijah, using the very verb of that verse, who told Israel scornfully to be one thing or the other, and not go limping along in impossible compromise (1 Kings **18**.21). Something like that had happened, it seems, to two Lycus Valley congregations, or Laodicea would not have been addressed in a word-picture derived from the geology or geography of the neighbouring thermal spa. We say goodbye to the congregations of John with this sad picture of easy-going worldliness. The letter from Patmos must have come as a shock.

## Questions and themes for study and discussion on Studies 59–62

1. How can a church be caught sleeping?
2. What 'open doors' are we prone to overlook today?
3. Is the Laodicean attitude still with us?
4. Why is 'lukewarmness' useless?

# THE LAST THINGS

## Judgement in the Teaching of the Apostles

### 63 : God Has a Day

### Acts 17.22–34

On his second missionary journey, Paul came to Athens, which could be called the greatest university centre in the Roman Empire. How would he preach the Gospel to Greek intellectuals? The text mentions the presence of Greek Epicureans and Stoics (17.18). The Epicureans had as their goal the freeing of men from fear of the ancient Greek gods which they considered to be the chief evil in life. They believed that the gods existed but that they had no concern for human affairs. The chief end of life was the pursuit of pleasure. The soul of man is material consisting of fine atoms distributed throughout the body, which dispersed at death. Thus the Epicureans had no idea of a substantial afterlife and no fear of death.

The Stoics thought the deity was a fine, invisible, fiery vapour which interpenetrated all the world and all living creatures, being the soul of man. At death, the soul was merged in the divine fiery essence of which they were sparks, and was believed to be born again and again through a hopeless succession of identical reincarnations.

Some have felt that Paul softened his message at Athens by not preaching the cross. The opposite is true. To be sure, Paul cited words from a Stoic poet which agreed with Christian thought, viz. that all men are the offspring of God by virtue of creation. But Paul taught three doctrines that were highly offensive to his hearers: that men were responsible to God; that men would have to answer to God in the day of judgement; that this judgement would be carried out by a man whom God has appointed and 'given assurance to all men by raising him from the dead' (31). Judgement and resurrection: these are two themes that neither Stoics nor Epicureans could fit into their philosophy. Thus it is clear that Paul was not trying to argue the philosophers into the Kingdom of God by the power of his reason: he was rather witnessing to the reality of God, judgement and resurrection. So must we.

## 64 : The Light of Nature

### Romans 1.18–32

In the first section of Romans (1.18–3.20) Paul expounds the *need* of God's salvation. All men stand before God convicted as guilty sinners, and therefore fall under God's righteous wrath (1.18). The wrath of God in the Bible is not so much an emotion like our human anger when we encounter frustration; it is the set attitude of God's holy will against the ungodliness and unrighteousness of men. It should be obvious that if God's Kingdom is to prevail, all that opposes His holy will must be removed; otherwise ungodliness and wickedness survive for ever.

God's judgement however is not arbitrary, but will be carried out in terms of every man's reaction to the light he has. Jews will be judged by the law; Gentiles will not be judged by the law (2.12) but on the basis of the revelation available to them.

In this first chapter, Paul argues that there is a revelation of God in nature, so that Gentiles are without excuse for their ungodliness. 'What can be known about God' from nature 'is plain to them, because God has shown it to them' (1.19), i.e. revealed it to them. Ever since the world was created, there are certain realities about God which can be clearly seen in the things that have been made; viz. God's eternal power and deity. Nature speaks of the 'godhead' of God and of His power. Paul does not say that this revelation is adequate to accomplish man's salvation. He does say that it is enough to make a man responsible to God to recognize that there is a God and to praise Him as such. Because they have not done this but have 'exchanged the glory of the immortal God for images resembling mortal man or birds or animals or reptiles' (1.23), God has given them up to all sorts of wickedness. 'So they are without excuse' (1.20).

## 65 : The Light of Conscience

### Romans 2.1–16

Men cannot escape the judgement of God by condemning others for things of which they are themselves guilty (2.1). Here is a familiar human technique. Someone has called it 'status by negation'. When my wife criticizes me for some act that displeases her, how easy it is to defend myself by answering, 'Yes, but I didn't do so-and-so like you did.' It is easy to defend oneself by trying to put down another.

However, God 'will render to every man according to his works' (2.6). Paul goes on to affirm that the Gentiles have an added source of the knowledge of good and evil—the light of conscience. Sometimes Gentiles who do not have the law of Moses 'do by nature what the law requires' (2.14). Even Gentiles recognize that such sins as murder are wrong. All people have a sense of right and wrong. Every people, however primitive, have their moral and ethical standards, however diverse they may be. Conscience is one of the gifts God gave man when He created him in His own image. When Gentiles follow the right as their conscience leads them, 'they show that what the law requires is written on their hearts' (2.15). Paul neither says nor implies that conscience is an all-sufficient guide. Neither does he say that men can be saved by obeying their conscience. In 1 Tim. 4.2 he speaks of a conscience that has been seared, i.e. rendered callous and unresponsive. His argument in Romans is that Gentiles will be judged, not by the law which they do not have, but by the knowledge of good and evil which they have in their conscience. They are responsible to God. We all are.

## 66 : Saved as by Fire

### 1 Corinthians 3.10–17

A day of judgement awaits not only unbelievers, whether Jew or Gentile, but also Christians, especially Christian leaders. The church in Corinth was in danger of dividing around human personalities who had visited Corinth—Peter, Apollos, Paul (1.12). Others, perhaps the most self-righteous of all, said, 'We do not trust human leaders; we follow only Christ.' The Corinthian church was in danger of breaking up into several factions.

Verse 5 makes it clear that Paul is discussing the role and work of Christian leaders in the church, particularly of himself and Apollos. He first affirms an obvious truth. The only foundation for building the Church is Christ. Different workers may legitimately build in different ways, but if a worker does not build upon Jesus Christ, his building is in vain.

However, not all build well, even when they build on Christ. Some build a structure which can be likened to a building of gold, silver and jewels—a beautiful permanent structure. Others build of wood, hay, stubble—materials which will not long endure. Paul says that the day of judgement will test every man's work by fire. The fire is not punitive but testing. Some buildings will be consumed; others will stand the test and survive.

Then Paul makes an important statement: 'If any man's work is burned up, he will suffer loss' of his reward from the hand of God; 'though he himself will be saved, but only as through fire', for salvation is altogether a matter of grace, not of works. Those whose works survive will receive rewards from the hand of God.

Verses 16, 17 are sobering words. From the context of the Corinthian situation, Paul is thinking of the local church as a holy temple. Since it is God's temple, if anyone destroys this temple by factious and schismatic conduct, he will incur God's judgement.

## 67: Who Know Not God

### 2 Thessalonians 1.3–12

We who live in 'Christian countries' are inclined to take our Christian faith for granted. We are never really persecuted because we are disciples of Jesus; in fact, many people determine their church affiliation in terms of social and economic standing.

Not so in Thessalonica, and not so in much of the 'non-Christian' world today, where it is still costly to be a Christian. When Paul came to Thessalonica, he first went to the Jewish synagogue, as his custom was, preaching for three weeks with considerable success (Acts 17.1–4). However, many of the Jews were angered and were able through mob violence to accomplish Paul's expulsion (Acts 17.5–10). It is clear that Paul's departure did not allay Jewish hostility, for the believers in Thessalonica have endured persecutions and afflictions (2 Thess. 1.4).

What will be the fate of those who 'do not know God and . . . who do not obey the gospel of our Lord Jesus' (1.8)? The revelation of Christ from heaven in a theophany of flaming fire (see Exod. 3.2; 19.18; Deut. 5.4; Isa. 66.15) will be a day of judgement for them when God will repay with affliction those who have afflicted His people. That day—the day of the return of Christ—will mean rest for those afflicted for Christ's sake, but 'the punishment of eternal destruction' for those who afflict

God's people. This could sound like the punishment of annihilation; but destruction may not mean destruction of life itself but of all that makes life worth living. This is more precisely defined in the phrase, 'exclusion from the presence of the Lord and from the glory of his might' (1.9). This is the same judgement expressed more than once by our Lord: 'I never knew you; depart from me' (Matt. 7.23); 'I do not know you' (Matt. 25.12). Is this not a just 'repayment'—God giving men what they have asked for? They have refused to know God in this life; He will refuse to know them in the life to come. On the other hand, for those who have responded to Him in love and obedience, He will come 'to be glorified in his saints, and to be marvelled at in all who have believed' (1.10). Is it not a just thing that God should give us what we have asked for—life in God's presence or loss in exclusion from Him?

## 68 : Believing a Lie

### 2 Thessalonians 2.1–12

In two of our earlier chapters (see Dan. 7 and 11), we found prophecies of an evil personage who will arise in the end-time to try to frustrate the work of God. This 'antichrist' also appears in Matt. 24 as the desolating sacrilege. In our present chapter, we have Paul's version of this same evil personage.

Paul calls him 'the man of lawlessness' (3) because he opposes and exalts himself against the law of God. Paul does not emphasize one of the main points found in Daniel and Matthew, viz. that the Antichrist will wage a violent persecution against the people of God. Paul places the emphasis upon two facts: he will be satanically inspired (9); and he will demand the worship of men. This is the meaning of the phrase 'he takes his seat in the temple of God, proclaiming himself to be God' (4). He will attempt to exercise religious totalitarianism—the deification of the state. Probably this is an allusion to the ambitions of the tyrant in Isa. 14.13 who said, 'I will ascend to heaven; . . . I will set my throne on high; . . . I will make myself like the Most High.' His appearance will be the signal for a widespread rebellion against God (3), apparently in dependence upon Antichrist.

Paul says that the man of lawlessness is being restrained at the present time; but when the restrainer is removed, the man of lawlessness will be revealed (7). This is one of the most difficult verses in the New Testament to interpret, for we have no record of Paul's previous instruction to the Thessalonians which this passage presupposes (5). The oldest interpretation finds its clue in the word 'lawlessness'. Rom. 13 tells us human government is divinely ordained to preserve law and order—to reward the good and to punish the evil. When human government fulfils its function, it restrains evil. It keeps lawlessness in check. Paul sees a day when government based on God's law will break down, totalitarianism will prevail, and men will be rewarded for evil—worshipping the state personified in the Antichrist—and punished for good—worshipping God. That which God designed to be an agency for good becomes a demonic power.

The reign of Antichrist will be short. 'The Lord Jesus will slay him with the breath of his mouth and destroy him by his appearing and his coming' (8). When this last outbreak of demonic evil has been subdued, God's people will inherit the Kingdom of God (1.5). God will have the last word.


# 69 : Preaching to Spirits in Prison

## 1 Peter 3.18–4.6

This is a notoriously difficult passage. It is probably better to capitalize 'Spirit' in v. 18 as does the Authorized Version (KJV); otherwise we have the idea of a resurrection of the spirit instead of the body—an idea which is elsewhere opposed in the New Testament (2 Tim. 2.18). The whole Christ was put to death in the flesh; the whole Christ was made alive in the Spirit. This same idea is found in Rom. 1.3f. The preaching to the spirits in prison has been interpreted in two different ways, and it is almost impossible to decide which is better. Many reformers held that in His pre-existent state, Christ preached the gospel through Noah to men in bondage to sin. The more widely accepted view today is that after His death, Christ proclaimed to the spirit-world His victory over sin and death. These spirits are usually understood to be the fallen angels ('sons of God') of Gen. 6.1–4. It would contradict the whole tenor of Scripture to hold that Christ extended to these spirits in prison the offer of salvation. The statement in 4.6 does not refer to this same event. There is no hint in Scripture that after death there is a second chance to hear the gospel and find salvation. 'The dead' are those who have recently died. Those who have died were judged in the flesh like men by suffering physical death, but because the gospel was preached to them while they were alive and could respond, they are now living in the spirit like God. Men need to hear the gospel while they are still alive.

# 70 : Scoffing at His Coming

## 2 Peter 3.1–13

It is clear that 2 Peter is much later than many of the other New Testament epistles. Paul constantly writes in expectation of the near return of the Lord. By the time 2 Peter was written, many years had passed, and men could point to the fact that many have died but 'all things have continued as they were from the beginning of creation' (3.4). No great event such as the return of Christ had occurred to interrupt the unbroken flow of events. Then the promise of Christ's return must be a vain promise.

Peter answers by two arguments. First is the argument from the flood. The earth, which was formed out of water (Gen. 1.9), was nevertheless judged by the deluge of the flood. Implied is the idea that the judgement of the flood did not happen at once, but in God's own time. In the same way, the present earth is reserved for a judgement of fire.

Peter's second argument is that God's time is not man's time. What is delay to man is not to God. In fact, God delays His judgement to give man time to repent.

In God's own time, judgement will fall. In this case, Peter says that judgement will mean the dissolution of the elements of the universe and then recreation to form new heavens and a new earth 'in which righteousness dwells'. The Bible paints the picture of the future with different colours. Sometimes the picture is very 'this-worldly' (see Amos 9.13); sometimes it is a new and different order (see Study No. 6 on Isa. 65, 66); but it is always a picture of a redeemed earth. The new order shares both similarity and dissimilarity with the old order. Sometimes, the element of similarity is stressed; sometimes, the degree of dissimilarity. The latter is the emphasis of 2 Peter. The old order must be dissolved, but not in order to discard it, but in order to see a new order emerge. It is new heavens and a new *earth* that we await (13).

This expectation should be an incentive to holy living (11). We are not only to wait for the arrival of 'the day of God,' we are actually to hasten its coming. The best commentary on this is the words of Jesus: 'This gospel of the kingdom will be preached throughout the whole world, as a testimony to all nations; and then the end will come' (Matt. **24**.14). He taught us to pray, 'Thy kingdom come' (Matt. **6**.10). By faithful prayer and extending the gospel in all the world, we hasten the return of our Lord.

## Questions and themes for study and discussion on Studies 63–70

1. Can you win a sceptic by the power of rational argument, or by Spirit-used witness to Christ?
2. Is the argument for the existence of God from order and design in nature an effective one today? Has modern science in any way disproved the orderliness of nature?
3. Do you think you have ever known anyone who has completely obeyed his conscience? Have you?
4. Does God give His servants rewards because their good works have put God in their debt? See Luke **17**.10.
5. Where in our generation have we seen the emergence of totalitarianism with a claim to complete allegiance almost divine?
6. Is it the *fact* of the approaching day of God or its *imminence* to which Peter appeals as a motive for holy living?

# CHARACTER STUDIES

## 71 : The Four Horsemen

### Revelation 6.1–8; 9.13–21

No one interpretation of this book of poetic prophecy precludes other modes of exegesis. The visions are fixed to no dates, and can have multiple fulfilment. The seven churches were real churches. They are also typical churches, and are found functioning today.

So with the Four Horsemen. As always the shortest path and the surest to meaning and understanding is to ask what John had in mind when he first wrote, and it seems clear that the struggles between Rome and Parthia, that great, unsolved problem of the north-eastern frontier, are prominent in John's mind.

Parthia was the successor state of the Persian Empire, and her mounted bowmen had struck heavy blows at Rome. Here, surely, was a vision of the Persian Shah, now represented by the Parthian monarch, who always wore white. A common title of the kings of the East was 'the Conqueror'. Mars, or Ares, god of war, follows in the guise of a swordsman on a crimson steed. Perhaps he has no particular nationality. The Parthians were bowmen, the Romans were men of the sword. Perhaps this is the clash of armies in some eastern Armageddon, with the most certain sufferers those whose land was trampled into infertile mud, and drenched in blood as defender clashed with raider.

A third horseman follows close behind (5). The horseman is famine, and his horse is black like the emaciated corpses by the stricken roadway. Famine follows war and breakdown. A denarius a quart was twelve times the usual market price for wheat, the vital commodity of life. In the midst of such starvation oil and wine remain mockingly unharmed. They are not dependent on a yearly sowing neglected in times of trouble. The vines and olive trees are not so easily trampled by the passing hosts. Last in the vision comes a pale or livid horse, the colour of a corpse long dead (8). The picture is strife among hungry multitudes, disease stalking abroad, the very beasts slinking into abandoned and undefended villages to rend the weak and the dying. The dreadful portrait of the rider on the pale horse is an inclusive vision. All the ills of his predecessors, after war's

cumulative fashion, are summed up in him. He is general chaos . . .
Such vision found widening fulfilment over the coming five
centuries. Like the world today, Rome lived behind frontiers of
fear. Nor has the moral law changed, nor the judgement which
follows rejection of God. The four horsemen, like Satan, are
'characters of Scripture' which we shrink from meeting. None the
less, they ride forth.


## *72 : The Martyred

### Revelation 6.9–17; Psalm 79.5–10

The martyred dead must surely find a place among the characters
of this book. The opening movement of the chapter presented in
poetic language an all too familiar sequence of social breakdown
and disaster. The latter half (9–17) takes the scene poetically to
heaven, in order to link the catastrophes of earth to the divine
judgement which permits them. The 'souls under the altar' call
for God's retribution on sin, cruelty and murder. It is easy for
the comfortable and secure to comment adversely on the cry of
the agonized, but let it be boldly said that, although the Christian
is bidden pray for his enemies, there is nothing wrong in com-
mitting the hardened and determined persecutor to God's
judgement and mercy, and to beg for an end to man's wickedness
to man.

Judgement is sure, and it is pictured under the sixth seal in the
imagery of Nature's violence, and of political anarchy. We saw
such use of the terrors of earth and sky in Amos, Joel, Isaiah
and Ezekiel. This was familiar symbolism to those whose whole
education was their ancient Scriptures. Nor has scientific
explanation robbed the earthquake of its terror, or the plunging
meteor of its majesty and might. The poet seeks language
adequate to bring to minds habituated to the picture-language of
the East the fact which still stands true—'it is a fearful thing to
fall into the hands of the living God', as the writer to the Hebrews
remarked. And here, in fact, another Character, One who has
haunted our every page enters the scene. Before perfect Goodness,
in the presence of Intelligence and Strength quite unimaginably
mighty, how pathetic is the strutting of captains and kings, how
feeble the little bombastic words of man, how pathetic his claims
to eminence, and how ridiculous his self-assertion (15–17)! And
in the light of Eternity how transient is evil! But if Christian men

endure, their sufferings are not in vain. They become part of the meaning of the Cross. They fuse their sacrifice with Christ's. As Lowell wrote a century ago:

> Careless seems the great Avenger; history's pages but record
> One death-grapple in the darkness 'twixt old systems and the
>     Word:
> Truth forever on the scaffold, Wrong forever on the throne,—
> Yet that scaffold sways the future, and, behind the dim unknown,
> Standeth God within the shadow, keeping watch above His own.

## *73 : The Redeemed and Their Lord

### Revelation 7

The strange catalogue of the sealed remnant of the tribes must be read in the light of the fact that the Church regarded the whole Christian community as the new Israel (Rom. 2.28f; Gal. 6.16; Phil. 3.3). Nor, in a book of symbolic language, can the numbers be taken literally, as some interpreters have often striven to do. The number twelve has significance in both Testaments. The square, twelve times twelve, multiplied a thousandfold, represents a perfect multitude, a generous rather than a niggardly total. In v. 9 the 144,000 merge with the multitude beyond all counting. These are they whom we have been meeting throughout this series of studies—they and their posterity.

The beautiful description of the reward from God's hand for those who came triumphantly out of great tribulation is one of the tenderest passages in the book. There is no need at all to limit the reference to any one tribulation, or to a great and final tribulation. There has been no generation, from the first century until today, when at least one portion of the Church has not faced, for the testimony of Christ, persecution and suffering which its victims must have looked upon as the ultimate in horror. John's word of comfort is for them all, and in such spirit those who suffer for the Name have always used it.

It was the thought of Christ's own sacrifice (14), which nerved and strengthened the conquerors to go through the fires and emerge to victory. It is to a sharp consciousness that they were treading a path which He had trod before, that the 'overcomers' owe their power to endure. Calvary again takes its place as the heart of Christianity. And see v. 17. It is the Lamb which 'shepherds' them, for the Lamb of this imagery is also the Good

Shepherd, and the image of His guidance and care is one which runs from end to end of the Bible. Grief, in that final day, will end, for there is no sorrow there. Note, too, that the apostle speaks of tears. The Lord was no hard Stoic; He wept at Lazarus' tomb. There is no virtue in proud unwillingness to weep. It is the task of Christlikeness to take away the tears of others, or to share them, as Jesus did. And how truly John saw God in what he had seen of Christ.

# 74 : The Dark Invaders

## Revelation 9

The reference to the river Euphrates, which was the lamentably insecure demarcation of the north-east frontier of the Empire, adds a strong likelihood to the suggestion that the plague which was unleashed against the eastern provinces was an inroad of mounted Parthian bowmen. The vast numbers mentioned (16) must be read in the context of apocalyptic poetry, for the whole population of Asia at the time did not amount to 200,000,000, the figure mentioned. Perhaps in the prophetic telescoping of time, the insight of the writer had in view the whole coming pageant of history's later catastrophes. All the riders from the untamed steppes, and the distant Gobi pasturelands, whence Hun, Mongol and Turk were yet to pour, are envisaged in one scene and moment of prophetic vision pouring in—a murdering, trampling multitude flooding through that one, wide disastrously gaping frontier. The sanguinary campaign of A.D. 58 to 62 against the Parthians must have filled the more exposed lands of the Middle East with tales of barbaric power beyond the Mesopotamian rivers. Plutarch, who wrote in the early years of the next century, spoke of the coloured and fearsome appearance of the Medes and Scythians, horse-riding tribes associated with the wild raiders, but there is no need, in such a context of apocalyptic imagery, to insist upon an allegorical meaning for every detail, much less to see a literal prophecy of arms and explosive weaponry, fortunately not known at the time when the words were written. It is the general impression which must be assessed, and that is one of stark and exotic horror. An ordered society is overrun and trampled by a foreign host. At the same time, it is possible to see historic fact in such details as those of v. 19. The Parthian bowmen were adepts at turning in the saddle of a galloping horse, and loosing a final volley of shafts as they withdrew at full speed from a rallying enemy. Hence the proverbial 'Parthian shot'. For all the storm of catastrophe, the evil society under attack and menace does not repent. The choice of Barabbas presses hard. They had chosen Caesar and rejected Christ.

## 75 : The Beast

### Revelation 13.1-10; Daniel 7

Chapter 13 of the Apocalypse is another illustration of the fact that no single interpretation of that strange book excludes the others. The vision of the Beast is poetry of the sort which the modern world, bemused by the imitators of T. S. Eliot, finds familiar. Let it also be granted that the chapter admits of historical interpretation for it is possible to set John's imagery in a context of history. And for those who find a 'futurist' interpretation attractive, there is the patent fact that the present century knows well enough the Beast that has cursed the past, the tyrant who demands the allegiance of hand and head. He would be optimist indeed who should say that the world has seen the last of the grisly procession.

The Beast came out of the sea, and that is an image in Scripture for the agitated mass of mankind which, as Victor Hugo put it in a strange poem, casts up grim creatures in times of crisis. 'The wicked,' said Isaiah, 'are like the tossing sea, for it cannot rest, and its waters toss up mire and dirt' (Isa. 57.20). And hear George Adam Smith's rendering of the same prophet's earlier word: 'Ah, the booming of the peoples, like the booming of the sea . . . like the rushing of many waters they rush . . .' John sees, like some galley of the imperial fleet showing sail, then dark hull, then pagan figurehead over the western horizon, rise up the Animal, first crowned horns, then head, then feet.

This most mysterious character of Scripture is a composite creation. Leopard, bear and lion, all of which strong beasts lived in Palestine, united to give it the symbols of cruelty, agility, craft, speed and power. It was Rome to which the East, along with its visible heads, the emperors, gave worship in temple and shrine, for Rome's rough hand had brought peace. Men, weary of war, worshipped Rome, and gave Rome and her princes 'names of blasphemy', the divine titles of the emperors common enough in John's own Ephesus.

Not counting Domitian under whom he suffered, and who still lived, there had been seven emperors, from Augustus to the short-lived Titus, or ten if the few weeks of Galba, Otho and Vitellius, the victims of the Year of the Four Emperors, A.D. 69, are counted. That was the year Nero died, and Rome bled in multiple civil war, almost wounded to death, but 'recovered of her deadly wound'.

## 76 : The Second Beast

### Revelation 13.11–17; Romans 13.1–7; Matthew 13.24–30; 1 Peter 2.13–17

The second Beast, the other composite character in this chapter, rose out of the land, a fierce Animal with a deceptive look of suavity. This surely is the religious hierarchy of Asia, and perhaps the local Roman governors, who could be coerced into the rigid application of the law. The law was on the books, and if the authorities saw fit to put John out of the way, they were also empowered to persecute with severity. A generation after this letter was written, Pliny, the humane governor of Bithynia, was told by Trajan, a just and able emperor, that the law was the law. The correspondence survives and illustrates v. 15. The governor describes his procedure: 'Those who denied they were, or had ever been, Christians, who repeated after me an invocation to the gods, and offered adoration, with wine and frankincense, to your image, which I had ordered to be brought for that purpose, together with those of the gods, and who finally cursed Christ—none of which acts, it is said, those who are really Christians can be forced into performing—those I thought it proper to discharge. Others who were named by an informer at first confessed themselves Christians, and then denied it; true, they had been of that persuasion, but they had quitted it, some three years, others many years, and a few as much as twenty-five years ago. They all worshipped your statue and the images of the gods, and cursed Christ.'

For those prepared to accept the writ of the authorities and in the same act repudiate Christ, a certificate could be issued, perhaps a seal and an official's signature on a document of repudiation. Nineteen such documents were discovered in 1904 and 1907 at the site of Theadelphia in Egypt. This is what the Aurelian family signed with appropriate witnesses: 'To the superintendents of offerings and sacrifices at the city. From Aurelius . . . son of Theodorius and Pantonymis of the said city. It has ever been my custom to make sacrifices and pour libations to the gods, and now also I have, in your presence in accordance with the commandment, poured libations, made sacrifice, and tasted the offerings, together with my son Aurelius Dioscuros and my daughter Aurelia Lais. I therefore request you to certify my statement.'

It is a sad document but illustrates the work of the second Animal.


## 77 : Man of Sin

### Revelation 13.17, 18; 2 Thessalonians 2

Grim régimes, in past centuries and ours, have known this apparition, the Beast clothed in authority that stamps a mark on head and hand, and denies a man a right to live unless he bows and worships. Things had changed in Rome since Paul bade Christians obey and act as good citizens should (Rom. 13.1–7), and since Peter bade men honour the Emperor (1 Pet. 2.13–17). Caesar-worship had changed it all. Rome was out to crush the faith and to demand the soul of man.

Hence the image of the seal. There is evidence of branding and tattooing of slaves. There was also a red seal bearing the emperor's name and effigy, which was used in documents of exchange. It was a sign of contract and in the metaphor of the chapter suggests acceptance of the Animal's law and authority.

And what of the last enigma: '. . . his number is six hundred and sixty-six'? Note first that some good manuscripts give 616, not 666. In both Greek and Latin the letters of the alphabet had numerical value, and the fact was commonly used to build puzzles. Among the wall scratchings from Pompeii is an election notice in which the vowels are exchanged for numbers, and another inscription speaks of a girl called Harmonia. 'The number of her name,' it says, 'is 45.' The key to the puzzle seems to be that Harmonia suggests the nine Muses, and 45 is the sum of all the digits from 1 to 9.

The churches of Asia probably knew the key to 666 or 616, but it was early forgotten. In Greek 616 adds up to 'Caesar God', but 666 is not so simple, and much ingenuity with spelling has been employed to fit the number to 'Nero Caesar', or 'Caius Caesar'.

It is also plausibly suggested that 666 falls short of the perfect trinity 777 in all counts, and thus presents a grisly picture of the power and baseness of Antichrist. The subject remains open for ingenuity. After all, the writer warns his readers: 'Behold, here is wisdom.' Perhaps some papyrus scrap, still undiscovered, some inscription under a Turkish doorstep or embedded in a wall, contains an answer to John's cryptogram.

But the vision abides among the dark shapes which form the characters of this part of Revelation—a thing of horror which has been seen and could be seen again.

## Questions and themes for study and discussion on Studies 71–77

1. Do the horsemen still ride?
2. Lowell's verse (Study No. 72).
3. How does the modern Christian 'overcome'?
4. The fragility of ordered society.
5. The Beast today.
6. How is Christ still repudiated?
7. 'Caesar-worship' in its modern guise.

# THE LAST THINGS

## The Consummation of the Divine Purpose

### Introduction

As already noted, a popular Christian idea of the final destiny of the saved is that when we die, we go to heaven. As a matter of fact, the New Testament has very little to say about the state of the dead in Christ. Paul does say that to be 'away from the body' in death is to be 'at home with the Lord' (2 Cor. **5**.8), and because of the many sufferings he has endured as a missionary, he has a desire 'to depart and be with Christ' (Phil. **1**.23). However, this existence of the soul with Christ after death is not the goal of salvation; it is an intermediate state awaiting the return of the Lord, the resurrection of the body, and the gathering of the redeemed in the Kingdom of God. The Christian hope is not primarily that of the salvation of the individual soul; it is the gathering of the people of God under God's reign, with every enemy destroyed, to enjoy the fullness of the divine blessings.

### 78 : All Israel Saved

#### Romans 11

We have seen in the earliest sections of this book that the Old Testament constantly views the coming of the Kingdom of God in terms of national, theocratic Israel. Jesus changed this. Entrance into the Kingdom of God would not be determined by membership in the nation Israel but only by personal relationship to Himself. This means that in terms of New Testament thought, the Church has replaced Israel as the people of God. In fact, the Church is the true Israel. It is men of faith who are the true sons of Abraham (Gal. **3**.7). Circumcision is no longer an act in the flesh but in the heart (Rom. **2**.28f.).

Does this mean that God has cast away His people, Israel, and supplanted them by another people (Rom. **11**.1)? This is the problem Paul discusses in Romans **9–11**. Is God all done with literal Israel? Paul's first answer is that within the Church, there is a believing remnant of Jews (1–6), a minority who have come to faith in Christ. The majority were hardened in unbelief (7-10). Have the majority stumbled so as to fall (11)? Is God's purpose fulfilled in their unbelief? On the contrary, God has a greater purpose; He has used the unbelief of the Jews to bring salvation to the Gentiles (11f.). Furthermore, God's final purpose is not found in their failure; they remain a 'holy' people—an object of God's particular concern (16).

Then Paul uses the famous figure of the olive tree—the people of God. Natural branches (Jews) were broken off because of unbelief and wild branches (Gentiles) were grafted in. However, the natural branches will be grafted back in if they do not remain in unbelief (23f.). Here is a new revelation of divine truth—a mystery (25). A hardening has come upon a part—indeed, a greater part —of Israel until God's purpose for the salvation of the Gentiles is fulfilled. Then Israel will come to faith, be grafted back onto the olive tree, 'and so all Israel will be saved' (26).

There is a clear statement that the consummation of God's redemptive purpose includes the salvation of literal Israel— the Jewish people. How or by what means or precisely when this salvation will occur Paul does not say. It can be called an 'eschatological event', for it is a part of God's plan for the consummation. Of one thing we are sure; the salvation of Israel must be in terms of faith in Jesus Christ as their crucified and risen Messiah, for there is salvation in no other name. Therefore, one cannot say from the New Testament that the present restoration of Israel as a nation is a sure sign of the end. The sign will be the salvation of Israel by faith.


## 79 : The New World

### Matthew 19.23–30

A young man once asked Jesus how to attain eternal life (Matt. 19.16). By this question, he was not thinking of eternal life as a present possession (see Study 41 on John 5.19-29); he was thinking of the life of the resurrection as taught by Dan. 12.2. In reply, Jesus speaks about entering the Kingdom of God, entering the Kingdom of Heaven, being saved, and the coming of the new world. All of these are interchangeable expressions for the final consummation which will occur after the coming of the Son of Man. The Kingdom of God means the perfected, unhindered rule of God; salvation is from death, mortality and all evil; the new world is another expression for the new heavens and the new earth discussed in an earlier section. Jesus' statement that it is easier for a camel to go through the eye of a needle than for a rich man to enter the Kingdom of God is not to be softened or watered down; it is a human impossibility. Only a miracle of God can change the affections of a rich man (or of a poor man either) so that he will love God and seek His Kingdom first. 'With God all things are possible.' The word translated 'new world' is literally 'regeneration' and refers to the regeneration of the world which will introduce the new redeemed order. The parallel passage in Mark 10.30 says, 'in the age to come (they shall receive) eternal life.' This implies resurrection. Eternal life belongs to the age to come—the future world. It means that mortality will be swallowed up by life (2 Cor. 5.4). The form in Matthew refers to the fact that Israel is finally to be saved and have her place in the Kingdom of God (see above, Rom. 9–11). The disciples will share with the Son of Man the privilege of ruling over the redeemed people of God.

## 80 : Freed from Decay

### Romans 8.18–25

Paul contrasts the sufferings of this present life with the glories of the world to come. He has just contrasted earthly suffering with Christ with the heavenly glory (17) and he apparently refers to the sufferings believers undergo because they are Christians. They suffer as Christ suffered—at the hands of their enemies. In the present passage, Paul refers more to the sufferings that befall all men, including the redeemed, because of the curse of sin on all creation. Because of the curse, 'creation was subjected to futility' (20). This means that the created world in and of itself is going nowhere. There are forces of evil and negation in the world which prevent it from achieving its proper end. The whole creation groans in travail together until now (22). It groans because of cruelty; it groans under natural disasters; it groans under the burden of decay and death. Even believers who have received the initial instalment of salvation in the indwelling of the Holy Spirit groan inwardly. Although our spirits have been made alive, our bodies are dying (Rom. 8.10). Those who have received the initial gift of life are not delivered from physical weakness, weariness, sickness, infection and finally death. So we groan, awaiting the resurrection, which means not merely the salvation of the soul but the redemption and transformation of the body. This is the glory to be revealed in the Day of the Lord.

Creation joins the saints in eagerly longing for this day when the resurrection will reveal who are the sons of God, because creation will share in this redemption. The created world will be delivered from its bondage to decay and death. This is Paul's way of describing what was called the 'regeneration' in the last section. Creation will share the glory of the redeemed saints. In this hope—of the redemption of both the created world and the physical outward life of believers—we were saved. It is now only an object of hope. We cannot see it; in fact, we can hardly imagine what it will be like. But we wait in hope that God will fulfil His redemptive purpose both for the Church and for the created world.

## 81 : All Things Subject to Him

### 1 Corinthians 15.21–28

There are two human families: the family of Adam and the family of Christ. As all who are in Adam inherit Adam's death and die as Adam died, so all who are in Christ will inherit Christ's life and in the resurrection will be made alive to live as the risen Christ lives. The resurrection is to occur in several stages, the first of which is the resurrection of Christ. His resurrection was not an isolated event. It was not the return of a dead man to earthly life. It was the beginning—the first fruits—of the resurrection which belongs at the end of this world and the beginning of the Age to Come. This means that a piece of the Age to Come—an eschatological event—the first instalment of the final resurrection—has occurred in the midst of history. This is why the Christian is sure of the resurrection at the last day—because this event has already begun to unfold. The first act of the drama has taken place.

The second act will be the resurrection of those who are in Christ at His Parousia or Second Coming. After that comes the end—the consummation of God's redemptive plan. The consummation means the final establishment of the Kingdom of God—His rule—in a rebellious world. At His exaltation, Christ began His reign at the right hand of the Father (Heb. **1**.3; Acts **2**.30f). He entered in upon His messianic rule as Lord and

Christ (Acts 2.36). In some way which Scripture does not disclose to us, He is to reign at God's right hand until He has made all His enemies a stool for His feet (Acts 2.34). When He has thus established His reign in the universe, He will deliver the Kingdom to God the Father. In the present passage, it is clear that these enemies are primarily spiritual powers, for 'the last enemy to be destroyed is death' (26). What comfort and courage Christians in an evil world should take to realize that, in spite of all appearances to the contrary, Christ is the Lord and is reigning at God's right hand evermore. This can be known only by faith. Confession that God had raised Jesus from the dead and made Him Lord was the central confession of faith in New Testament times (Rom. 10.9). The Second Coming or Parousia of Christ will be the revealing to the world of what the Christian already knows to be true: Jesus is Lord. Then, every tongue shall confess that Jesus is Lord and every knee bow before Him—willingly or of necessity (Phil. 2.10). He whom we now confess to be Lord will in fact at the consummation become openly Lord of all the world. When this has been accomplished, He will restore the Kingdom to God and will become Himself subject to the Father, His messianic work successfully accomplished.

## 82 : Lord of All

### Philippians 2.1–11

This is the greatest Christological passage in the entire Scripture. Paul writes about Christ, not as an end in itself, but because of the practical value of his doctrine of Christ. Christians are not to try to snatch honour and recognition from others in the interest of self-aggrandizement. Rather, Paul urges the Philippian believers to follow Christ's example of self-abnegation, and leave to God the matter of bestowing honour.

Here is a clear affirmation of the pre-existence of Christ: 'he was in the form of God'. The best commentary on this is Jesus' prayer in John 17.5: 'Father, glorify thou me in thy own presence with the glory which I had with thee before the world was made.' In the Old Testament visitation of God, glory was often the physical manifestation of the presence of God. When Solomon dedicated the temple to God, the glory of the Lord so filled the house that the priests could not enter it (2 Chron. 7.2). Before He lived on earth, Jesus not only existed with the Father; He also shared the very form of God's self-manifestation. In the Old Testament, however, the existence of God as the triune One—Father, Son and Holy Spirit—was not yet revealed. Men knew only God—Yahweh. In the Old Testament, the Spirit is sometimes personified but never personalized. The Spirit of Yahweh is God's power at work in the world—thus God Himself. Thus in the Old Testament, men knew and served only God the Father, not the Son.

Although He had a right to universal honour and worship as the eternal Son of God, Jesus did not snatch at it like a robber snatches booty (see AV[KJV]'s 'robbery'); on the contrary, He took the way of self-abnegation by emptying Himself—pouring Himself out. This He did in His incarnation when He took the form of a servant and was born in human form. As if this wasn't enough, He humbled Himself to the lowest death, even death on a cross. God in turn has bestowed on Jesus the rank He refused to snatch for Himself—*Kyrios*, Lord. God has exalted Him to heaven, seated Him at His right hand, and given Him the name of absolute sovereignty—Lord. When His lordship is complete, every knee will bow and every tongue confess that Jesus is Lord. This does not mean universal salvation; it does mean that in the end, at the consummation, every hostile will will be subordinated to the will of Christ, the Lord.

## Questions and themes for study and discussion on Studies 78–82

1. In light of Rom. **11,** can the Christian tolerate any trace of anti-Semitism?
2. What conclusion do you draw about possible difference or similarity in meaning in the expressions, 'Kingdom of God/Heaven' from Matthew **19.**23f.? Compare with Mark **10.**23f.
3. Does Rom. **8** teach that the more evil we experience in this life, the more glory in the future life? Is there merit in suffering?
4. Can one *prove* that Jesus is Lord from the events of human history?
5. How can Paul believe that Jesus *is* Lord and at the same time call Satan the 'god of this age' (2 Cor. **4.**4)?
6. Aside from the lordship of Christ, do we have any assurance that history has any ultimate meaning or goal?

# CHARACTER STUDIES

## *83 : Rome in Triumph

### Revelation 17

Rome was a personality in John's day, a dark 'character of the Bible'. Apart from personification which made the Babylon of the New Testament a person of evil, a blood-drunken woman throned on her seven hills, Rome was worshipped, along with the emperor, in temples of the Caesar cult. John's searing denunciation of the evil creature was a lone voice. Rome had given peace to those who accepted her stern rule, and war-weary men saw her as the only hope as the frontiers bent under the pressure of an alien and uncivilized world.

Quotation can proceed until the final break-down. Here, for example, is the Greek rhetorician Publius Aelius Aristeides. He writes of Rome in the middle of the second century:

'You have made one single household of the whole inhabited world. Before the establishment of your empire, the world was in confusion, upside down, adrift, out of control: but as soon as you Romans intervened, the turmoil of factions ceased, and life and politics were illuminated by the dawn of an era of universal order ... so that today the earth and all that dwell therein are endowed with a clear and comprehensive security.'

Claudian of Alexandria writes with no less enthusiasm at the turn of the grim fourth century:

'Rome alone has taken the conquered to her bosom, and has made them to be one household with one name—herself their mother, not their empress—and has called her subjects citizens, and has linked far places in a bond of duty. Hers is that large loyalty to which we owe it that the stranger walks in a strange land as if it were his own; that men change their homes; that it is a pastime to visit Thule and to explore mysteries at which once we shuddered; that we drink at will the waters of the Rhone and the Orontes; that the whole earth is one people.'

Or hear a Gaul, Claudius Rutilius Namatianus, writing astonishingly in A.D. 416, six years after Alaric's sack of Rome:

'You made one fatherland for varied races, and under your

rule it was advantage for those who willed it not to be taken, and in offering the conquered a share in your own law, you made a city of what was once a world.'

By this time the Empire had surrendered, too late to save herself. The capital had changed to Byzantium in the East, and it was there, Constantinople as he now named it, that Constantine established Christianity as the official cult. The Roman Peace had its vast advantages. During its high noon Christianity was established. Then the Empire turned on the force which might have changed her life. Christians must have felt bitterly lonely in the midst of the chorus of adulation and of praise. Christians feel lonely still in the midst of the praise for the world of collapsing values today. But the laws of history stand.

## *84 : Rome in Ruin

### Revelation 18

The tone changes. This chapter is less apocalyptic in its imagery, but Rome is still a personified reality. It required a bold prophet to see beyond the two centuries of prosperity and peace within the bounds of Empire which lay ahead and write this grim 'taunt-song'. The deluded world laments its overturned idol. The merchants bewail its passing. Perhaps in some Asian port John had watched the galleys loading their cargoes, redolent of the wealth sucked from a subject world by the Beast by the Tiber. There was 'merchandise of gold and silver and precious stones, of pearls and of fine linen, and purple and silk, and scarlet cloth, and vases of ivory, and costly wood, and of brass, and iron. There was cinnamon, and perfumes, and ointments, frankincense, and wine and oil ... fine flour, and wheat, and horses, sheep, chariots, and slaves, AND SOULS OF MEN.'

The climax was bitter, and came last to the watcher's lips as he turned away from the loading dock. The Seer knew that, unless all history lied, Rome would pay for the last-named cargo in blood and ruin. And he seemed in the foresight of his vision to see the port of Ostia in the ruin in which it stands today, its warehouses hollow shells, Rome under the smoke of her burning and the voices of her music stilled. So Nineveh had lain of old under Nahum's contempt, and Tyre under Ezekiel's scorn. And here now was an audacity of prophecy to outdo them all. The Seer saw a vast world empire doomed for persecution's sake, consigned to nether Hell because she had drunk the blood of the ones who had wished her well and who had spoken the words which might have saved her.

How that prophecy turned into dark fact is a matter of history. The fall of the Roman Empire is a horror which has, until today, held the fascinated imagination of the world. Rome had her opportunity, as the peoples of a wider global society have today. In the fateful generation which lay between Nero and Domitian the voice of Christianity became clear and vocal. Rome could have made her saving choice. But Rome, like a vicious person chose evilly and paid the price, over four centuries of revolution, tension, tyranny and final dissolution. So it happens with nations —and with men.

## 85 : The Conqueror

### Revelation 19

It is important to place this imagery of the mounted Conqueror in its proper context of thought. John is not reverting to the Jewish notion of a warlike Messiah marching to free the nation or people of His choice from the bondage of the oppressor. Those who walked with Christ had expected such a consummation, even in the days when they were with their Master in His lowliness. It is clear from the Gospel narratives that they looked upon those days as a time of preparation and disguise, out of which the Conqueror of their dreams and expectations would, at the proper moment, arise. Even after His resurrection they could still ask: 'Lord, will You at this time restore the Kingdom to Israel?' (Acts 1.6). John had been sufficiently instructed in the nature of the Kingdom, and the reality of his Lord's Messiahship, not to imagine that the discarded misconception of a militaristic, nationalistic kingdom could in any way be revived.

We are reading the language of poetry, and the imagery of soldiering for Christ was used by Paul in writing to Ephesus, and in his last word to Timothy. It is found in many hymns. John is merely summing up the whole message of his book. He has seen the dawning of God's triumph over evil. The 'many waters' is an image from the opening vision of the book. The noise of the sea, driven by the north wind is seldom absent from the Aegean islands. God's voice in John's rich imagination sounded like the unending roar or murmur of the surf, but rose at times to the crash and roll of the thunder. So, in John's vision, was the utterance of God, always speaking for those who listen, but at times rising in the din of storm.

And now the glorified Christ rides forth to final victory. It is a demonstration of the old exile's indomitable faith that God and good will prevail. He is showing us that all evil must die, that sin contains the certainty of its own destruction, that tyranny is doomed, and judgement sure upon rebellion. 'Wherefore, let us this day, take up the whole armour of God, that we may be able to stand in the evil day, and having done all to stand' (Eph. **6**.13). We are a vanguard of the host. A vital skirmish may be ours.


## 86 : The Dead

### Revelation 20.11–15; 22.11; 2 Corinthians 5.10; John 3.18, 36

The awesome scene of the Great White Throne shows the ultimate ordering of justice in the similitude of a mighty court before a Judge who never errs. There is a strangely terrible saying in **22**.11 which suggests that it is part of our human responsibility to carry into eternity the choice we make in time. We carry our own condemnation. 'Time present and time past,' said T. S. Eliot, 'are both perhaps present in time future.' Choose evil now and that choice is projected into another life. Choose death now, and death abides our lot. Dante, amid the sombre horrors of his poem, touched the edge of that truth: 'And I looked and saw a whirling banner which ran so fast that it seemed as if it could never make a stand, and behind it came so long a train of people that I should never have believed death had undone so many. And I saw and knew the shade of him who from cowardice had made the great refusal, and with certainty I perceived that this was the worthless crew that is hateful to God and His enemies, wretches who were never alive . . .'

Such was the poet's judgement on uncommitted lives. They followed a banner of swirling mist and had never really lived. Like the hand on Belshazzar's wall, we write our own doom. If the verb for 'perish' in John 3.16 is taken, as it can equally be, in the middle voice rather than the passive, that famous text can read '. . . that whoever believes in him should not destroy himself but share the life of God'.

114

At the great assize which John pictures the sentence of condemnation, self-chosen and self-willed is merely confirmed. Condemnation is mere confrontation with self.

> *I sat alone with my Conscience,*
> *In a place where time had ceased,*
> *And we talked of my former living,*
> *In the land where the years increased,*
> *And the ghosts of forgotten actions*
> *Came floating before my sight,*
> *And things that I thought were dead things*
> *Were alive with a terrible might.*
> *So I sit alone with my Conscience,*
> *In the place where the years increase,*
> *I seek to remember the Future,*
> *In the place where time shall cease.*
> *For I know of a future judgement*
> *Whatever that judgement be;*
> *That to sit alone with my Conscience*
> *Will be judgement enough for me.*

## 87 : 'I Jesus'

### Revelation 22

The vision is over. The book is ended. John has seen his Master again arrayed as he had never seen Him before, save in that brief transfiguration flash of another world on the slopes of Hermon, almost a lifetime before. The island of exile resumed its daily shapes and colours—the two harbours almost cutting its mass in half, the small white town huddling by the sheltered water's edge, the vine-clad and olive-clustered slopes, the vast sweep of the sea, gold in the sloping sun.

His Lord, he knew, had always been with him. Such indeed had been His promise, and the last of the Lord's men knew that, in all life's experience, that promise had held true. He was still with him at the book's end, as at its beginning, with him for evermore.

We who have moved during these studies through the Bible, looking at the men and women who made it, whose sins and sorrows, joys and virtues fill its pages, are conscious of that other presence. There was Another with the three young men in the furnace (Dan. 3.25), 'and the form of the fourth was like the Son of God'. It is typical.

Foreshadowed in the Old Testament, a reality in the Gospels, a risen Lord in the story of the Church and in the experience of the writers of the New Testament, the Other in the story has always been at hand. Was there ever One so to dominate the writings of men? The writings only? He dominates the life. He is the supreme Character of Scripture. He is the Christian's everpresent Lord, his Word, his Will, all life's 'magnificent obsession'.

'Behold, I come quickly' . . . And the promise holds when the fight is hard with foemen 'leaning on our shield' and 'roaring on us as we reel', when the way is dark and His purpose elusive, when earthly hopes fade, friends fall by the way, and likewise when the sun is on the road and 'heaven above a softer blue'. 'Even so come, Lord Jesus. Make haste to save us.'

And the grace of our Lord Jesus Christ be with you all. Amen.

## Questions and themes for study and discussion on Studies 83–87

1. Why was John so lonely a voice?
2. Do the rules of history still work?
3. Is the Second Coming preached enough?
4. Why is lack of committal so deadly?
5. How do *you* sum up all these studies?

# THE LAST THINGS

## Revelation

## Introduction

The last book in the Bible is the Revelation of John, and it differs from most of the other books in that it is 'apocalyptic' (see the chapter on Daniel). We have seen that while both the prophets of the Old Testament and the New Testament writers are much concerned about the future, the Revelation is altogether concerned with future events which 'must soon take place' (Rev. 1.1). The difference is one of emphasis and not of kind, for the entire New Testament bears witness to the fact that God's redemptive work is as yet incomplete. Without the Second Coming of Christ, resurrection and judgement, the Kingdom of God remains a hope and a dream. Revelation makes extensive use of symbolic language and, to us, fantastic imagery. Because of this symbolism, it is difficult to interpret, and no book of the Bible has been subject to such diverse interpretations as this one. We take it to be a true prophecy (1.3) of the events that will attend the end and the coming of God's Kingdom.

(The final series of biographical and of doctrinal studies both come to their climax in the Book of the Revelation. This was inevitable, but it does involve some little overlap. Where this is so, however, each of the two writers concerned has approached the passages with a different emphasis (and at times with slight differences of interpretation), and the studies should prove complementary to each other.)

## 88 : The Glorified Christ

### Revelation 1

The Revelation is addressed to seven specific historical churches in Asia Minor (1.4); and chs. 2, 3 are seven letters addressed to each of these seven churches. In the Revelation, numbers almost always have a symbolic quality. We do not know why these particular seven churches were selected; we know of other churches in Asia Minor. But seven is symbolic of fullness. These seven churches represent the total Church; and therefore the Revelation is addressed to all Christians. However, initially, it was designed to be read aloud in the public worship of these seven churches.

Tradition tells us that John lived to a ripe old age in Ephesus. At this time, he had been exiled to a small barren island in the Mediterranean called Patmos (9). We have no other information about this exile; but it is clear that it was punishment for being a Christian.

One Sunday (on the Lord's day) John was 'in the Spirit' (10). In Paul, to be 'in the Spirit' is the state of all Christians (Rom. 8.9)—the sphere in which they live their lives. In the Revelation, it designates entrance into an ecstatic state in which he could receive a vision from the Lord (see 4.2; 17.3; 21.10. See also 2 Cor. 12.2; Acts 11.5; 22.17). His first vision was that of the risen, ascended, glorified Lord, standing in the midst of seven golden lampstands, which represent the seven churches. His white hair represents deity (cf. Dan. 7.9). His feet like burnished bronze symbolize judgement. The sharp sword proceeding from His mouth, represents the Word of God (Heb. 4.12). The seven stars in His right hand, which represent the angels of the seven churches, is difficult, but probably symbolizes the heavenly character of the Church. The glorified Christ then dictates to John the seven letters which John wrote down and later sent to the seven churches, together with the visions which he saw of the events of the end.

*The Christ we worship is glorious and awe-inspiring, but He also calms the fears of His trusting people.*


## 89 : The Lion is the Lamb

### Revelation 4 and 5

John received the seven letters to the seven churches 'in the Spirit', i.e. in a trance. Again, he found himself a second time 'in the Spirit', and he was caught up in vision and carried as through an open door in the sky into heaven. There he saw God seated upon His throne. However, he gives no description of deity, except the beauty of precious stones. Seated on twenty-four thrones around God's throne were twenty-four angelic beings who are pictured as assisting God in His administration of the universe (see Psa. 89.7; Isa. 24.23; I Kings 22.19)—a counterpart to the elders in

Israel (Exod. 24.9–11). Around the throne were seen four creatures who combined features of the Old Testament seraphim of Isa. 6.1–3 and the cherubim of Ezek. 10.14, who may be conceived of as guardians of God's holiness.

Then John saw in God's right hand a book in the form of a scroll sealed down the outside edge by seven seals, effectively closing the scroll from any human eye. The scroll is the book of the consummation of God's saving purpose—the goal of redemptive history. John is told that only the 'Lion of the tribe of Judah, the Root of David' can break the seals and open the book, i.e. bring forth the judgements and the salvation of the end. By these symbols we are reminded of the Davidic King of Isa. 11 who will 'smite the earth with the rod of his mouth, and with the breath of his lips he shall slay the wicked' (Isa. 11.4).

When John looked to see the conquering lion, he saw a lamb with its throat cut from sacrifice, nevertheless standing on its feet. It went to the throne and took the scroll from the hand of God and prepared to open it. In this way, John links together Jesus' redeeming and His conquering work. Only because He is the slain Lamb of God—only because of His sufferings and death on the cross is He able to bring history to the Kingdom of God. Here is mystery. The cross is not only atoning and redeeming; it is conquering. Only because He is the Lamb of God can He become the King of kings.


## 90 : Safe and Secure

### Revelation 7

As John in vision stands on the threshold of the last period in history preceding the return of the Lord, called in Matt. 24.21 the Great Tribulation, he sees in vision two throngs: one of 144,000 of the twelve tribes of Israel, and a great innumerable multitude. He first sees four angels at the four corners of the earth holding back the judgements of God until God's servants have been sealed. Then he sees 12,000 of each of the twelve tribes of Israel sealed upon their foreheads with the seal of God. The purpose of this sealing does not appear in this chapter. It emerges in 9.4 where the 144,000 are shielded from the judgements of God. During the Great Tribulation, two great movements are taking place: the effort of the Beast to destroy the Church by giving believers the option of worshipping the Beast

119

or suffering martyrdom (see ch. **13**), and the divine judgements poured out by God upon the Beast and his supporters (**16**.2). These judgements are represented by the seven trumpets (chs. **8, 9**) and the seven bowls (ch. **16**). These judgements are not only punitive but have the ultimate purpose of driving men to repentance before it is too late (**9**.20; **16**.10). During these terrible days the people of God will find themselves in the midst of an apostate people, but they will be sheltered from the divine wrath. We are reminded of Israelites living in Egypt who were shielded from the ten plagues which fell on the Egyptians.

The difficult question arises: are these literal Jews picturing the salvation of Israel (see Rom. **11**) or not? One fact stands forth: these are in no way the twelve literal tribes of Israel. Nowhere in the Bible can this listing be found. Dan is omitted; Ephraim is also omitted but is included indirectly because Joseph was the father of both Ephraim and Manasseh. This means that in reality Manasseh is included twice. Can this be John's way of representing Israel which is not *literal* Israel? Such a distinction is made in **2**.9 and **3**.9. If so, this pictures the Church in the tribulation sheltered from the wrath of God. The symbolism of $12 \times 12,000$ represents the intact preservation of the people of God. They are spiritually safe; Satan cannot destroy Jesus' Church. They will be brought safe and secure through the tribulation.

This does not mean preservation from tribulation and persecution. The second group is the same people as the 144,000, this time pictured as having passed through the Great Tribulation and standing safe and secure before the throne of God. This does not mean preservation from martyrdom; it does mean spiritual security. God will save His people.


## 91 : War in Heaven

### Revelation 12.1–17

This chapter provides us with the key to the whole structure of New Testament thought leading up to the consummation. Behind the scenes of human history is being waged a mighty spiritual battle between the Kingdom of God and the kingdom of Satan. Jesus' most characteristic miracle was that of delivering men from satanic evil in the form of demon possession. This was a sign of the presence of the Kingdom of God (Matt. **12**.28). In fact, it was the power of God's rule present in Jesus which effected this miracle. Jesus further describes His mission as that of invading a strong man's house—Satan's realm—and plundering his goods—delivering demon-possessed people. This could be done only because He had *first* bound the strong man (Matt. 12.29). It is the mission of the Kingdom of God in Jesus' ministry to despoil Satan's realm.

This same truth is presented in the present chapter in a drama painted in colours of mythological symbolism: a war between a fierce red dragon and Michael's hosts of angels. The identity of the woman clothed with the sun is a bit difficult. She may represent Israel, but more probably the heavenly Zion, the mother of us all (Gal. 4.26), and so perhaps the people of God of every age. As such she includes Israel. As she gives birth to Messiah, the dragon tries to destroy Him, but He is caught up to God (5). This is not meant to represent Jesus' ascension, for there is no mention of His death and resurrection. It is simply a vivid way of describing Messiah's protection from Satan.

In the war between the dragon and Michael which follows, the dragon was overthrown and cast down to earth. Some take this to refer to an actual spiritual battle to take place in the end time. If so, this is the only reference to such a battle, and its meaning is difficult. It is better therefore to take it as a symbolic picture of Jesus' victory over Satan referred to above, even though here it is Michael who does the fighting. In Luke 10.18, referring to His victory over Satan, Jesus said, 'I saw Satan fall like lightning from heaven.' Because Satan has been overthrown and knows his time is short, he comes to earth with great wrath (12) to try to destroy the people of God. This is described symbolically as his pursuit of the woman, but he is unable to overcome her. 'Then the dragon was angry with the woman and went off to make war on the rest of her offspring' (17), the empirical Church on earth. 'And he (the dragon) stood on the sand of the sea' to call up from its waters the Beast—the Antichrist—in a final attempt to destroy the Church.

*In every age, including our own, the struggle of Satan against the Church is fierce—but futile.*

## 92 : The Two Beasts
### Revelation 13.1–18

We have already seen in the studies on Dan. 11, Matt. 24 and 2 Thess. 2 that the Bible sees the age-long struggle between the

Kingdom of God and the kingdom of Satan to concentrate in the end times in an evil individual—the Antichrist. He is the first beast of Rev. **13**. He is called up from the sea by Satan. His appearance is a synthesis of the four beasts of Dan. **7**, and represents a final apostate civilization. The Revelation, like Paul in 2 Thess. **2**, indicates that he is satanically inspired, and that he demands the worship of men (4). The blasphemy which he utters against God (6) does not mean cursing God; it means desecrating the divine name and violating His glory and deity by demanding the reverence from men which is due only to God. This is what Paul meant when he said that the man of lawlessness would take his seat in the temple of God (2 Thess. **2**.4). Satan would destroy the Church through the Antichrist by turning the loyalty of men from Christ to Antichrist. Here is the issue: Christ or Antichrist? It is the eternal destiny of men that is at stake. The demand for worship is seen in the mission of the second beast which is portrayed in colours of the ancient state cult of the worship of Rome, practised in Asia Minor. His one purpose is to make men give their loyalty and worship to the satanic Beast. Here is totalitarianism; political, religious and also economic (11–17).

The Beast is allowed to persecute the saints. Persecution in the New Testament is represented as the normal expectation of Jesus' disciples. To be His follower means to be willing to go to martyrdom as Jesus did. Nothing less than this is the meaning of taking up one's cross (Mark **8**.34). In the world we are to expect tribulation (John **16**.33). Only through much tribulation can we enter the Kingdom of God (Acts **14**.22). This tribulation, which is the normal expectation of the Church throughout the age, comes to its climax in the persecution of the Antichrist. However, the difference is quantitative and not qualitative. 'It was allowed to make war on the saints and to conquer them' (7) in martyrdom. However, in reality, the martyrs have conquered the Beast (**15**.2) for they had not denied their Lord. In fact, *their very martyrdom was their victory*.


## 93 : The Marriage Supper of the Lamb

### Revelation 19.6–21

Chapters **19–22** form a connected narrative which pictures the actual consummation. Chapter **19** pictures three things: an announcement of the marriage supper of the Lamb, the return of Christ, and the judgement of the Beast.

The wedding feast is not described; it is only announced. It takes place after the return of Christ. The announcement in v. 6 should be rendered, 'The Lord our God the Almighty has entered upon his reign.' This is a proleptic announcement of the consummation, which means negatively the judgement of evil and positively the salvation of God's people. This is pictured in terms of a wedding feast (see Matt. **22**.1–14; **25**.1–13). The Church is often pictured as the bride of Christ (2 Cor. **11**.2; Eph. **5**.25ff.), now betrothed to Him, awaiting full union at Christ's coming.

John then depicts the Second Coming of Christ. His whole concern is Christ as victor—Christ the conqueror of His enemies. The idea of Christ as the bridegroom of the Church is displaced by the idea of Christ the conqueror of the Antichrist and Satan. Therefore Christ is pictured in terms of an ancient warrior, riding a white horse to make war. His blood-stained robe has been thought by some to symbolize the blood of His cross. It is more likely that it represents the blood-stained garments of a warrior. He is accompanied by the armies of heaven, also arrayed in white; but we are not told that they join in the battle. His only weapon is His Word—a sword proceeding from His mouth. We are reminded of creation: God spoke, and it was done. In His final conquest, He will speak, and victory will be His. Here is infinite mystery. His name is the Faithful and True—He can be depended on to fulfil God's redemptive purpose. He also has a name which He Himself alone knows; the human mind cannot grasp the depth of His person.

The third section pictures the judgement of the Beast (17–21) in terms of the carnage of an ancient battle field. The birds of the air are summoned to gorge themselves on the carcasses of those who have given their allegiance to the Beast. The Beast and the false prophet were captured and thrown into the lake of fire; and those who had supported them were slain with the sword.

# 94 : The Millennium

## Revelation 20

Chapter **19** pictured the destruction of the Beast and the false prophet. This chapter continues the narrative to tell of the destruction of Satan, who stood behind the Beast. His destruction is pictured as occurring in two stages. First, he is bound with a chain in a 'bottomless pit' for a thousand years, 'that he should deceive the nations no more' during this period. After it, he is released and again deceives the nations to rebel against Christ. He is defeated, however, and then thrown into the lake of fire where the Beast and false prophet are.

This chapter also pictures the destruction of death. At the time of the binding of Satan occurs the 'first resurrection' (6), with special emphasis on the resurrection of the martyrs of the Beast. The rest of the dead do not come to life until after the thousand years. Then all the dead come to life and are judged by a twofold standard: by their works, and by the book of life. All whose names are not found in the book of life are cast into the lake of fire. Then, death and the grave are also thrown into the lake of fire.

This chapter has been the subject of great controversy and therefore we offer two different interpretations. The most natural interpretation is that there are two resurrections of the dead: of the saints, with special emphasis on the martyrs, before the millennium; and of the rest of the dead after the millennium. There are two stages in the conquest of Satan after the Second Coming of Christ. His power is curbed so that he will not deceive the nations during the thousand years. During this period of millennial bliss, Christ and His risen saints rule over the earth. In this case, the millennium is a real period of time between Christ's Parousia and the end when human history will experience unparalleled peace and prosperity, because Satan is bound, and Christ Himself reigns.

However, one must admit that this is the only place in the Bible which explicitly teaches such a millennial kingdom. Many Bible teachers, following the analogy of Scripture, feel that this passage must be interpreted in the light of Scripture as a whole. We have already seen that Jesus in His earthly ministry won a victory over Satan (see Study No. 91). These scholars therefore equate the binding of Satan in Rev. 20 with that alluded to in Matt. 12.29. Furthermore, the New Testament does teach a spiritual resurrection. 'The hour is coming, and now is, when the dead will hear the voice of the Son of God, and those who hear will live' (John 5.25). God has 'raised us up with him, and made us sit with him in the heavenly places in Christ Jesus' (Eph. 2.6). Such scholars equate the 'first resurrection' with the spiritual resurrection which occurs when one believes in Christ, and the second resurrection as the bodily resurrection at the end. In this case, the 'millennium' is a period symbolic of the whole Church age, and the reign of the 'resurrected' saints is either the spiritual reign of the saints with Christ (Eph. 2.6), or else it refers to the blessedness of the martyrs in the intermediate state. Contrary to appearance, they do not really die; they live in heaven and reign with Christ.

Whichever view is chosen, one thing is clear. In the end, Satan, death and the grave are destined to be cast into the lake of fire and be destroyed so that they destroy God's people no more.

## 95 : The City of God

### Revelation 21

This chapter teaches the same as 2 Peter 3.11–13 that the present heaven and earth are destined to be displaced by a new heaven and a new earth. However, the final destiny of the saints is a redeemed *earth*. The city of God, the new Jerusalem, comes down out of the heaven to the new earth. The final destiny of believers is not 'to die and go to heaven'; it is a new earth where heaven has come down to earth. The significance of this is that 'the dwelling of God is with men. He will dwell with them, and they shall be his people, and God himself will be with them' (3). 'They shall see his face' (22.4). These are the most sublime words in the Bible; this is the goal of all redemptive history. Previously, all knowledge of God has been a mediated knowledge. 'No one has ever seen God; the only Son, who is in the bosom of the Father, he has made him known' (John 1.18). In the consummation, there will be no more need of mediation. 'They shall see his face.' This is perfected communion and fellowship.

The city of God is described in obviously symbolic terms. It is pictured as cubical in shape: 1500 miles long, 1500 miles wide, 1500 miles high. What kind of elevators will they have in such a city? Obviously these dimensions represent the ideal symmetry, perfection, vastness, and completeness of the new Jerusalem. The walls are only 216 feet high—all out of proportion for such a mighty city. There are twelve gates bearing the names of the twelve tribes of Israel, and twelve foundations bearing the names of the twelve apostles. This signifies that the city will be the habitation of saints from both the old and the new dispensations. There was no temple in the city, for men have direct access to the Lord God and to the Lamb. Its glory will be such that it beggars the light of the sun, and in its light, the redeemed of the nations of earth shall walk.

Here is the fulfilment of our constant prayer; 'Thy kingdom come, thy will be done on earth as it is in heaven.'

## 96 : The River of Life

### Revelation 22

The first five verses of this chapter are a continuation of what has just preceded. John sees the river of life flowing from the throne of God through the middle of the street of the city. A moment's reflection shows that this is picturesque language denoting that the inhabitants of the city have entered into eternal life. It is impossible to take this literally and picture something like the streets of Amsterdam with their canals in the middle of the streets. Remember that this city is 1500 miles in size and cubical in dimension. Such a city would have hundreds of thousands of streets if not millions. We are reminded of the Old Testament prophecies of Ezek. **47** and Zech. **14**.8. In Ezekiel, a river flows from the door of the temple which is located not in Jerusalem but south of it (Ezek. **47**.8f.). The river flowed eastward towards the Dead Sea. In a third of a mile the river was ankle-deep; in another third, it was knee-deep; in a full mile it was waist-deep; in a mile and a third, it was so great one could not wade through it. What a marvellous river! How great would it be fifteen miles away from its source? In Zechariah, there are two rivers of living waters flowing *out of* Jerusalem: one flowed east and one flowed west. Obviously, both of these are picturesque ways of describing the future fertility of what was once wasteland.

John also sees the tree of life bearing twelve kinds of fruit—one each month. It is not the fruit that is life-giving: 'the leaves of the tree were for the healing of the nations.' Again we are reminded of the trees standing on the banks of the river in Ezek. **47**.12, which yield fresh fruit every month, whose fruit is for food and whose leaves are for healing. These are different pictures describing the same reality. In the consummation, there will be no sickness or bodily weakness. Mortality will be swallowed up by life.

The most important activity in the new earth is expressed in the words, 'his servants shall worship him'. Here is a sobering thought. Most people who have been reared in our 'Christian' world would express the hope that someday they will go to heaven and experience a blessed afterlife. But many of these same people have no taste for the worship of God. They are never found with the people of God on the Lord's Day. They live practically as though God did not exist. How could people who have no interest in worshipping God enjoy a life where the worship of God is the most characteristic activity? The chief end of man is to glorify God and enjoy Him for ever. Is that the chief goal of your life in this world?

### Questions and themes for study and discussion on Studies 88–96

1. Do not the pictures of Christ in Rev. **1** and in Rev. **4, 5** conflict with each other? Why not? How can Christ be so differently pictured?
2. What difference in interpretation of the identification of the twenty-four elders is determined by the different text in the AV(KJV) and the RSV at Rev. **5**.9f.?
3. What is the main activity of the twenty-four elders and the four creatures? What is the significance of this fact for us?
4. Compare the marriage feast in Rev. **19** with Jesus' words in Mark **14**.25.
5. What is the significance of the fact that Hell is pictured both as a place of fire and of 'outer darkness' (Matt. **8**.12; **22**.13; **25**.30)?
6. Should 'millennialism' ever be made a test of orthodox faith?
7. What need will the city of God have for a wall with gates?